UNLOCKING

THE

IDIOMS

To Gerald — from whom
I first learned about words
and great friendship,

George

UNLOCKING

THE

IDIOMS

AN LDS PERSPECTIVE
ON UNDERSTANDING
SCRIPTURAL IDIOMS

GEORGE M. PEACOCK

CFI
Springville, Utah

ISBN 13: 978-1-59955-241-5

Published by CFI, an imprint of Cedar Fort, Inc., 2373 W. 700 S., Springville, UT 84663
Distributed by Cedar Fort, Inc., www.cedarfort.com
LIBRARY OF CONGRESS CATALOGING-IN-PUBLICATION DATA

Peacock, George M. (George Morris)
  Unlocking the idioms : an LDS perspective on understanding scriptural
idioms / George M. Peacock.
    p. cm.
  Includes index.
  ISBN 978-1-59955-241-5
  1. Bible--Language, style. 2. Book of Mormon--Language, style. 3.
Doctrine and Covenants--Language, style. 4. Idioms. 5. English
language--Idioms. I. Title.

  BS537.P43 2009
  220.6'6--dc22

                          2009002825

Cover design by Angela D. Olsen
Cover design © 2009 by Lyle Mortimer
Edited and typeset by Heidi Doxey

Printed in the United States of America
10 9 8 7 6 5 4 3 2

Printed on acid-free paper

Also by George M. Peacock

UNLOCKING THE NUMBERS

TABLE OF CONTENTS

INTRODUCTION

I dioms and idiomatic language are as real to the messages of holy scripture as are prophecies and parables. Idioms are words and phrases that express more than the actual words themselves. They paint mental or emotional images that bring events or feelings to the present quickly and with intensity. They describe the way things are without using lengthy explanations. They do this by identifying the past experience of the reader or hearer and drawing upon his or her own feelings regarding the subject. Idioms are meaningless and can be misleading if the reader or hearer has no experience with the message being conveyed. "Take time to smell the roses" is such an idiom. The words say nothing about slowing down and appreciating what is around you. Furthermore, if you have never smelled roses or do not care for their aroma, this simple idiom will mean little to you.

Idioms are also obscured in their meaning. Like prophecies and parables, they cannot be understood if they have been translated poorly. Most expressions in the scriptures were originally written in languages unfamiliar to present readers. So dependence upon the work of translators is essential. Today the Christian world has many translations of the Bible from which to study and learn. Many of these translations have come forth since the authorized King James version was printed in 1611. These more recent translations resulted from translators using many of the same ancient texts, in addition to texts not readily available to the King James scholars. These other translators have sought the same objective as those authorized by King James. However, there is an impressive consensus that the King James version is one of the most literal translations into English. The King James translators operated under the design of word for word translation. Whereas other modern translations, such as the New Inspired Version (NIV), use equivalent figures of speech in English to translate many biblical words and phrases. This does not make the King James Bible less true; however, it does require the reader of that translation to be more aware of the meanings of biblical expressions because of its more literal rendering. If readers are not aware of these differences, they will be much more prone to miss the messages intended by the figurative terms. They will be confused by the expressions and forms of speech that were used in the original documents that did not survive through the translation process.

Some idioms are timeless. They fit any period of our existence. "He asked for her hand" is one of these. In most cultures a prospective groom must ask the prospective bride, or someone who is responsible for her, for permission to marry her. To ask for her hand gives a message much different than to ask for her ear or her foot. It has a connotation of being together and sharing, of leading, and of helping. It suggests, among many other possible ideas, reaching out to one another. But they all can be said by the simple phrase of "asked for her hand."

Other idioms are time specific. "He's using plastic" had no meaning until just decades ago. The term "9/11" had no significance until September 11, 2001. For those who were involved in that tragedy or who had family or associates involved, it means something different than to those who were not involved.

"I'll drop a dime on you" used to be a threat to tell the police about something illegal you had done. Now, it means little to a criminal because it costs far more to make a phone call than just ten cents—finding a pay phone is nearly impossible. So that idiom is obscure to all except those who lived during the era of ten cent calls from pay phones.

Readers look for understanding, so whatever is read is interpreted according to the reader's culture and language. It should be very helpful to those who read scriptural documents to know that they are reading the writings of Eastern authors. These authors were reared in Eastern settings, spoke and wrote Eastern languages, and knew Eastern figures of expression. Not only were they totally immersed in Eastern culture, but they knew nothing of the approaching Western culture and society who now study their writings. If they could have been aware that their writings would be translated into Western languages, they may have chosen to not use so many figurative expressions. Comparisons easily indicate that the Eastern communicator is far more prone to articulate by using imagery created by words and phrases than is the Western communicator. Even though the Western culture today is teeming with new words and terms, invented by the hundreds each year, the proficiency of the Eastern mind to create figurative imagery is "ahead by a mile" or "out of sight" when compared to Western thinking.

This natural disadvantage inherent in the Western student of Eastern passages of scripture does not lessen the challenge. In fact, it intensifies it. Knowing that the last days are upon us, and also knowing that God has spoken anew from the heavens, obligation to know the "mind of God" and what was taught by his Only Begotten Son is more imperative than it ever has been. Today there are more tools available, than ever before, to assist in studying and registering these writings of prophets. Therefore, to remain unchanged in our perceptions of the past shows an unawareness of the disadvantage under which we study.

Some will think that they are betraying their parents and past teachers if they consider new concepts. But remember the outcome that resulted because Joseph Smith set aside old sectarian doctrines and studied Hebrew, Egyptian, German, and Latin texts. He corrected errors in the Bible and seemed to be fearless in adding new doctrine. His attitude in these matters should guide us faithfully in a quest to understand scriptural text. Prophets since Joseph have welcomed new understanding as well and have preached and taught the same.

Some scriptural students have chosen to cry out that the figurative viewpoint is the "easy way out," and hold to the literal wording that appears in their text. Examples are Jonah and the whale, Moses and the burning bush, and seeing the face of God. However, knowing that those who wrote and spoke were not telling myths or tales, but rather that they were using forms of expression that go beyond the actual words themselves is helpful. They were doing this in order to add meaning and initiate movement in the minds and hearts of those to whom they wrote and spoke. The same is true today. If you want to tell a lover how you feel, it might be all right to just say "I love you." But often the expression used is more like "I love you to death," "I love you to the moon and back," "You are the sunshine of my life, the air I breath," "I worship the ground under your feet," or "You are the wind beneath my wings." These phrases project images and feelings that go far beyond a simple expression of love.

IDENTIFYING IDIOMS

Idioms can be easily overlooked. First of all, they must be read within the context of the surrounding section. The subject of the text should be the first clue that certain words are figurative. If the words or elements do not fit or agree, then consider the possibility that figurative expressions are being used. If they have been translated literally, these words and phrases will seem impossible, irrational, or senseless. This alone should be a clue that the author of the passage was communicating something beyond the ordinary meaning of the words. This is an immediate clue that a figurative expression is in play.

For example, if someone is speaking about his house, but says that the "taxes are killing me," he is not speaking of death. He is using a figurative expression while speaking of the taxes on his house. The "killing me" phrase is to give intensity to the effect which the taxes are having on him.

Moses seeing a burning bush must be considered in light of God calling him to free his people from bondage in Egypt. The question of what a "bush," and especially a "burning bush," has to do with this call to Moses should be a clue to consider a figurative element. Such an element may be foreign to us today. However, we must look for expressions used in the days of Moses if we are to understand his writings. Such idioms, when identified, will cause us to say, "Oh, I see! That makes sense to me now."

Adam and Eve are discussed in the Genesis account relative to their disobedience to God's commands, when it is noted that they are "naked." The message of the text is regarding disobedience, not about being without clothes. We may assume that we know the meaning of "naked" and read on while making conclusions that will never be what was intended by the writer. Why, you ask? For the same reason that someone who is driving too fast will misunderstand, if they are stopped by a police officer, who asks, "Where's the fire?" If the driver has never heard or used the idiom "Where's the fire?" he will never be able to properly answer the officer. The driver will be saying to himself, "I don't know. I wasn't going to a fire. I am just late for an appointment." If we do not identify the idiomatic parts of the scriptures, we will not understand the message intended by the author.

Expressions identified as idioms can be literal or transparent. It is often difficult to know how to take the message of these sayings. Guiding principles such as context can help us. However, the most challenging task is identifying an idiom when it is in between the two extremes of literal and figurative. And there is a definite area between the two. Some have classified the in-between realm as semi-transparent and semi-opaque.

TRANSPARENT—SEMI-TRANSPARENT—SEMI-OPAQUE—OPAQUE

A literal idiom that is very transparent is easily understood. Such expressions as "they built a fire," "he cut himself," or "head of the family," fit this classification.

Expressions become metaphorical or semi-transparent when they can be taken both ways. Such as, "killing two birds with one stone," "add fuel to the fire," or "skating on thin ice." They could actually take place; however, they can also tell of a condition that is similar or comparative to the real thing.

Phrases that lean more to the opaque, and are not so clear as to their literalness, include "burned all his bridges," "paints everything with the same brush," or "now the shoe is on the other foot." Such statements could be identified as semi-opaque. They could remotely be possible, but not very likely. Therefore it would be wise to consider them to be more figurative.

Last is the category of expressions which are not possible but still are metaphorical. They move into the area of hyperbole. They exaggerate a real event and thereby communicate a message. Such sayings are opaque or not clear in their meaning unless one is enlightened and

knows the background or meaning of the idiom. Idioms in this category are ones like "jump down someone's throat," "roll over in his
grave," and "by the skin of his teeth."

Having some rules to employ when deciding the message of idioms
is helpful. Consider the following:

a) If the phrase is opaque or semi-opaque, first consider a figurative
   message.
b) If the phrase is surrounded or included among other idioms,
   first treat them all alike.
c) If the author is telling a metaphorical incident, then likely the
   idioms used will be metaphors. The converse of this rule should
   also be applied.
d) If the phrase is used elsewhere, let one usage guide you in
   considering the other.
e) If a phrase is used in a teaching environment, likely it will
   be metaphorical or figurative. That is how the most effective
   teaching is achieved.

HOW IDIOMS COME ABOUT

It is often easier to describe someone or something by comparing
that person or thing to some phenomenon that is well known to all. For
example, we can say, "She's drawn to him like a moth to a flame." By
using this figurative expression, no long description of her attraction
or peril needs to be made. Not only is the idiom short, but it likely says
something about the end result of the attraction. People seldom can
explain just why moths are drawn to a flame, but they have observed
that moths get too close to the flame and are mortally wounded. All
this can be said by the idiom without having to describe it in actual
words. There is also a mental image created of the moth coming to its
fate, and the woman's attraction is part of the mental association.

Historical events also lend to creating idioms like, "Your name
will be Mudd." Only those familiar with the assassination of President
Abraham Lincoln will catch the feel of such a statement. However, to
those who know that John Wilkes Booth fired the fatal shot into the
president, likely also know that Booth was assisted in his plot by a man
named Mudd. The members of the Mudd family were so humiliated

that they either changed their name or wanted to do so. Thus a use of the idiom tells of both fate and feelings.

(For more information about the origin of many common idioms see "Where Did That Come From?" in the appendix.)

TYPES OF IDIOMS

There are several forms of idioms. Likewise, idioms are only one form of figurative communication—others being parables, hyperboles, allegories, similes, and metaphors. But idioms take on the forms of hyperbole, euphemism, metonymy, metaphor, and personification. There are other sub-categories as well. However, the following are illustrated:

Hyperbole

Definition: An exaggeration to make or reinforce a point.

A modern example of an idiom classified as hyperbole would be: "That box you made me carry **weighed a ton**."

The idiom is trying to give an indication of the exertion and effort that was made in lifting the box, not how much the box actually weighed. Therefore the weight description is exaggerated.

A scriptural example of an idiom classified as hyperbole would be, "Jesus saith unto him, I say not unto thee, Until seven times: but, Until **seventy times seven**" (Matthew 18:22; emphasis added). Some will want to count the number of times they are to forgive, but Jesus' message goes far beyond any number and teaches the principle that we should always forgive.

Euphemism

Definition: The use of a culturally acceptable term or phrase in place of a vulgar or harsh one.

An example of an idiom classified as a euphemism would be, "She was in a **family way**, even though they were not married." For many, especially those living decades ago, the term *pregnant* was not a word to be used publicly. So they spoke of the condition in the kindest way possible.

A scriptural example is well known, "And [Joseph] knew her not till she had brought forth her firstborn son: and he called his name

JESUS" (Matthew 1:25; emphasis added). The idiom "knew her" is used as a euphemism in place of a sexual word.

Metonomy

Definition: A noun that is substituted for another noun because of its meaning coming from the same origin.

A modern example comes easily. It could be: "He sure got his **eyes opened** when he saw what we had done." The statement does not infer that he was going around without his eyes closed previously. A greater nuance was intended by using the idiom: the new revelation was so expanded to him that it was comparable to seeing with your eyes open instead of closed.

A scriptural example of metonymy in an idiom would be: "That the **sons of God** saw the **daughters of men** that they were fair; and they took them wives of all which they chose" (Genesis 6:2; emphasis added). This verse contains two idioms. "Sons of God" indicated men who were God's sons, but the idiom goes beyond that and indicates that they were holders of the priesthood (See D&C 84:34–35). The "daughters of men" tells us that even though these females had fathers who were men, they were not followers of God.

Metaphor

Definition: An implied comparison between two items done without the comparative words "like" or "as."

A modern example would be: "He's a fish out of water trying to do this job." A scriptural example is, "Ye are the **salt of the earth**: but if the salt have lost his savour, wherewith shall it be salted? it is thenceforth good for nothing, but to be cast out, and to be trodden under foot of men" (Matthew 5:13; emphasis added).

Personification

Definition: A phrase that amplifies a personal trait or characteristic beyond its inherent function.

Modern examples of an idiom which do this would be: "She ripped my heart out," or "he ripped me to shreds."

A scriptural idiom using personification is: "They wear **stiff necks** and **high heads**; yea, and because of pride, and wickedness, and abominations, and whoredoms, they have all gone astray save it be a few, who are the humble followers of Christ; nevertheless, they are led, that in many instances they do err because they are taught by the precepts of men" (2 Nephi 28:14; emphasis added).

If the translators did not recognize such figurative expressions and translated them literally, readers of their translations will have difficulty understanding the original intent of the author. Furthermore, if the translators did recognize and understand the idioms, but assumed that anyone who read their translation understood the idioms like they did, then those of us who read their translations will be "in the dark" if we no longer use such idioms. Either way, we as readers are likely at a disadvantage in understanding the meaning of what was originally written.

Skilled communicators use idioms both when they speak and when they write. Idioms let them speak to our emotions and communicate how things really are without multiplying words. Prophets have used idioms and they have learned the properness of this skill from God himself. Both anciently and in modern times God has spoken from the heavens and used idioms in his language when giving direction and expressing emotion to his prophets and children. When we read the scriptures, if we do not recognize these idioms or identify them for what they are, we will not feel the emotion that God or his prophets intended.

Objectives of This Book

It is the goal of this writing to identify idioms, words, phrases, and sayings, whose meanings are often undisclosed—sayings which are often overlooked because they are not understood. This book will give helpful explanations to explain or unlock their meanings. By reading this book, you will become more adept at recognizing figurative forms of speech when they appear. You will thus have a better chance of identifying the messages intended by the Lord and the scriptural authors. I hope this book will help you recognize and perceive forms of speech and customs that have changed between our own time and the time when they were first written. You then will be more prepared to note the idioms that have gone through translation from one language to another.

You will also be more prone to recognize the idioms used in modern revelations. You will do this, not only because you are more skilled, but also because many of the idioms from writings of the past are similar to those used in the latter days.

Authorities of the Church have provided some commentary on some of the idioms in this book. I am familiar with these commentaries; however, just because commentary has been given does not close the door to new understanding. New understanding regarding who can hold the priesthood, the work of various priesthood offices, temple ordinances, and numerous other practices and policies would never have come about if we had held to original commentary. Joseph Smith was always seeking clarification about and a better understanding of scripture. He sought out those who could read other languages into which the Bible had been translated so as to have a more clear understanding of the original texts.

It is not the intent of this writing to tear down previous commentaries. However, we are blessed today with numerous helps unavailable to those of the past. The biggest consideration in all of these commentaries is to look at the figurative manner of speech. A literal interpretation has been the accepted position for so much of scripture, yet we have revelation indicating that the Lord's manner of speaking is figurative. In instructions to the saints in Kirtland in 1831, he said, "These things are the things that ye must look for; and, **speaking after the manner of the Lord**, they are now nigh at hand, and in a time to come, even in the day of the coming of the Son of Man" (D&C 63:53; emphasis added). In that revelation appear such phrases as "die at the age of man," "they shall not sleep in the dust," "the twinkling of the eye," "until that hour," "there will be foolish virgins among the wise," and "I will send mine angels to pluck out the wicked and cast them into unquenchable fire." These are but a few idioms and sayings which we must understand if we are to understand the manner of the Lord's speaking. They are not literal but figurative.

This book does not include all idioms found in the scriptures. Such a compilation would be "bigger than the ocean." There are "millions of them." They are "everywhere" when you read. They are more numerous than "flies on a cow pie." However, this book will consider those idioms that are most commonly problematic to readers. I have also included many other idioms because I felt they would be of legitimate interest to readers. Some might think that I'm "barking up the wrong tree," or that I'm "just blowing smoke." But I can tell you that "I've worked my fingers to the bone" and "gone out on a limb" to try and write this compilation. If you enjoy it, I will be "in seventh heaven."

I hope the idioms in the previous paragraph have communicated something about this work and how I feel about it. These idioms would likely lose their messages if they were translated into another language or used in another culture. That is precisely what happened to many scriptural passages. They lost their figurative messages in time and translation. Explaining them would require long discussions. Scriptural authors did not take the time to explain the expressions they used. They wrote with the assumption that those who read would know their meaning. That was the challenge for Bible translators. The challenge to those of us who read their translations, as well as those of us who read modern revelations, is to distinguish the literal from the figurative. We have to know the long explanations. That is the challenge! That is what this book is all about. As one cowboy said, "This may be your first rodeo, but it ain't mine."

These explanations are not to be considered as doctrinal statements of The Church of Jesus Christ of Latter-day Saints. They are mine. I have listed sources for certain helps I have used. However, I hope that word definitions, modern-day expressions, and the scriptures themselves will be seen as the major contributors to the explanations given herein. Contradicting explanations are generally not stated for the very reason of avoiding conflict and argument. I hope you will appreciate the processes and helps given herein and consider them respectfully in regard to what others have opined. However, if something is not what was originally intended by the Lord or his servants, perpetuating it is not helpful. It is not good to build a "house of cards" that will someday not hold up. Therefore, these explanations are given with the objective in mind that we must do all that we can do to understand holy writ. That can only be done with an open mind and a thirst for truth.

Yes, opinions of scholars and prophets must be held in high esteem, but they have courageously given their interpretations based on these same platforms. When the Lord has spoken and defined principles and sayings, that is final and concrete. Other interpretations, even those given by prophets, are open to change. Peter, without change, would have the gospel taken only to the circumcised. Plural marriage would still be the practice of the Church without Wilford Woodruff's new understanding. And rebaptism would still be a practice to indicate rededication. These are but a few examples of change from prior teachings and understandings of prophets. When prophets have written on certain scriptural points, they have done so only after consulting opinions of scholars, both within and outside of the restored Church. Their opinions are "not to be sneezed at." However, their opinions are also not the doctrines of the Church if they are writing as individuals, and not as a part of their callings. I appreciate what they have written. However, what they wrote may well have been based on what they could see with the light available to them at the time. The same is true of this humble treatise.

IDIOMS MISUNDERSTOOD BECAUSE OF LITERAL TRANSLATION

"giants in the earth" Genesis 6:4

Having knowledge that there were large men, such as Goliath, in the Bible narrative naturally leads to forming that image in our minds when the word *giant* is used in scripture. However, reading the surrounding text in the chapter of Genesis that describes the command to Noah to build the ark, should be a clue as to what the concerns of God were regarding his people. He is not rejoicing that there are large men who could be used in constructing the ark. He is concerned with the wickedness that abounds and that this great wickedness has overcome those who were to have been mighty and to have led in righteousness. They have failed, and only Noah and his family were righteous. Today we know what sports reporters mean if a small school from Division II college athletics beats a "Michigan" in the top of Division I programs. They could be described as "giant slayers." Further, a Michigan-type school, with its enormous stadium is referred to as "the big house," and could be described as "head and shoulders" above most other schools. Such imagery helps the reader know the potential of these teams. Often a single man can be eulogized as being a "giant of a man." This does not refer to his physical size but to the nature of his character or potential. So in the record in Genesis, we should look for the same elements. The phrase "giants in the earth" is hyperbole and was not written to be taken literally. Because apostasy and disobedience prevailed in Noah's time there were giants of men who had fallen. The interpretive word from the Hebrew would be "fallen ones."

The Genesis account reads as follows: "There were **giants in the earth** in those days; and also after that, when the sons of God came in unto the daughters of men, and they bare children to them, the same became mighty men which were of old, men of renown" (Genesis 6:4; emphasis added).

The same account is recorded in the Joseph Smith translation and more information regarding the motives and nature of those called giants is noted. It reads: "And in those days there **were giants on the earth,** and they sought Noah to take away his life" (JST Genesis 8:6; emphasis added).

However, the most descriptive narrative comes in the Book of Moses regarding the subject of giants. It gives the motives of those giants, without an inference to their size, but does indicate how they were overcome and became fallen. This record states: "And in those days there were **giants on the earth**, and they sought Noah **to take away his life**; but the Lord was with Noah, and the **power of the Lord** was upon him" (Moses 8:18; emphasis added).

In his address at the funeral of President Gordon B. Hinckley, President Thomas S. Monson used a quote that had been used before in similar circumstances. He used a metaphor regarding giants, similar to the use of giants in Genesis. Speaking of President Hinckley, President Monson said, "quoting from the poet, here and there, now and then, God makes a giant among men." It is certain that no one who heard President Monson say that quote had any thoughts of the size and literal stature of President Hinckley. On the contrary, the message of the idiom was that President Hinckley had done works of giant proportion. It was a wonderful tribute, especially coming from a man who physically towers over nearly everyone who ever stands next to him. President Monson who most resembles a giant in size, but, like

President Hinckley, he will also be described as a giant because of what he has done and will do as he leads the Church on behalf of the Lord.

"cut down their groves" Exodus 34:13

This is an idiom which can best be described as semi-transparent—it can be taken both ways. It can be literal and can be also figurative. The difficulty understanding the phrase is because of a poor translation. The idiom sounds like someone cut down a nice grove of trees. But when you learn that the word *grove* was translated from the word *Asherah*, who was the most worshiped pagan fertility goddess, the mother of Baal, and abhorred by Jehovah, you acquire an idea of the significance of the idiom. The Lord demanded that the Israelites who were preparing to enter Canaan were to "destroy their altars, break their images, and **cut down their groves**" (Exodus 34:13; emphasis added). A more clear translation would have been "and cut down all the images of Asherah, also known by her plural name Ashtaroth." If the King James version read that way, this phrase would not be considered an idiom.

Since Asherah's name is associated with things "upright" such as groves, trees, and carved poles, she was naturally made out of wood, whereas, Baal, Chemosh, and several other gods were made of stone or cast metal. This is why you find instructions from the Lord that read, "But thus shall ye deal with them; ye shall destroy their altars, and break down their images, and cut down their groves, and burn their graven images with fire" (Deuteronomy 7:5).

Note the treatment given to images made of stone and the treatment also for the groves and graven images. The pattern in the Old Testament in dealing with idols is consistent. Observe how "Good King Asa," King of Judah, acted. "For he took away the altars of the strange gods, and the high places, and brake down the images, and cut down the groves" (2 Chronicles 14:3). Another young but righteous king named Josiah led this way, "And they brake down the altars of Baalim in his presence; and the images, that were on high above them, he cut down; and the groves, and the carved images, and the molten images, he brake in pieces, and made dust of them, and strowed it upon the graves of them that had sacrificed unto them" (2 Chronicles 34:4).

An illustration of why we should know this idiom is as follows: When Gideon was called by God to lead Israel away from the wicked ways of the Midianites and the Amalekites who had power over them, Gideon did a courageous thing under God's instruction. He threw down the altar, which his own father had built to Baal, and offered a sacrifice of his father's bullock to Jehovah on the spot. He was afraid to do it during daylight hours, so he did it by night. What he did was serious. But the next thing he did seems to read as only an act of vandalism. However, if the reader knows the idiom "cut down their groves," then what he did takes on real meaning, as does his father's defense in the verses that follow. (See Judges 6:25–32.)

"generation of . . . this generation" Matthew 23:33, 36

The word *generation* is often identified with having only one definition. It is thought of as the time between the birth of one person, or group of people, and that of their parents or their children. However, to understand many of God's words, we must know that "generation" or "this generation" means those that were generated. We speak of the new generation of hybrid automobiles that run on both fossil fuels and batteries. Or we note that today's business world contains a new generation of entrepreneurs. John the Baptist used this later definition when he compared the religious leaders of his time to vipers. "But when he saw many of the Pharisees and Sadducees come to his baptism, he said unto them, O **generation of vipers**, who hath warned you to flee from the wrath to come?" (Matthew 3:7; emphasis added). John the Baptist was not using the word *generation* to indicate children of a father or a number of years. He was speaking of those in a category that had been produced or generated into a certain classification. John was calling the Jewish leaders vipers because vipers are poisonous and therefore could kill the body. He was contriving a message that indicated the leaders would kill the soul in the same way vipers killed the body.

The Savior used the idiom **"this generation"** regarding the Jews. He said, "Verily I say unto you, All these things shall come upon **this generation**" (Matthew 23:36; emphasis added. See also JST Matthew 23:34–35). Many read this verse and feel that it is speaking only of those Jews of Jesus' day. However, in latter-day revelation, the same phrase appears, "And it shall come to pass, that **this generation** of Jews shall not pass away until every desolation which I have told you concerning them shall come to pass" (D&C 45:21; emphasis added. See also Matthew 24:34 with footnote).

To consider that the term generation is only referring to one period of time or from a father to his children is very misleading. When the expression "clean from the blood and sins of this generation" is used, people will often ask, "Is that our generation or some other generation?" Answer: neither. It is referencing those who have been generated through Adam. It is speaking of those who are of the same make and model as Adam.

In 1832, the Lord made a declaration which still applies today. He spoke, "That their souls may escape the wrath of God, the desolation of abomination which awaits the wicked, both in this world and in the world to come. Verily, I say unto you, let those who are not the first elders continue in the vineyard until the mouth of the Lord shall call them, for their time is not yet come; their garments are not clean from the blood of **this generation**" (D&C 88:85; emphasis added). Again, it is misleading to identify "this generation" as only those alive in 1832.

Another example of the word *generation* was used by the Savior as he taught regarding those who seek for signs. People who seek for signs have always existed, not just in Jesus' day. Jesus said, "A wicked and adulterous **generation** seeketh after a sign; and there shall no sign be given unto it, but the sign of the prophet Jonas. And he left them, and departed" (Matthew 16:4).

To be certain of what Jesus taught, we must not just think of the unbelieving Jews, but we must make certain that we will not generate ourselves into sign seekers. If we do, then we will be part of that generation because we will be part of that same make and model.

"dead bury the dead" Luke 9:59

Jesus made a statement to a man who wanted to follow and serve him in his work. The man only had one hesitation or concern. He asked if he could first go and "bury his father." The Savior's answer to him seems very insensitive. "Jesus said unto him, Let the **dead bury their dead**: but go thou and preach the kingdom of God" (Luke 9:59–60; emphasis added). Translators, not looking with a literal eye, now look at Aramaic words and see keys that should be considered. They see that Jesus was answering the man in the same manner as an employer today would speak to an employee whose father is very near dying. The employer would say something like: "You first bury your father, then we will get you back at your new assignment." His statement includes

15

both his father's ensuing death and also the son's need to see that he is buried properly.

Likewise, the Savior is not telling the man that he cannot take a few hours and bury his father. For during this era of civilization, burials took place soon after a person died. What Jesus is more likely telling the man, whose father is old, non-productive, and therefore considered "dead," is to let the community and his fellow associates, who likewise are "dead," assist the man's father to the end of his life and see that he is buried. The translation does not portray the Savior in his natural demeanor. Had the man's father actually just died, likely the Savior himself would have attended the burial as part of his work and compassionate love. Today someone may speak idiomatically and say, "First, let me get this project, which I'm working on, moved to the back burner and then I'll drop you a line." Try and find what was meant by that statement if you look at it literally! We should give both the man and the Savior some consideration and not take literally what either of them said.

"smite him with the tongue" Jeremiah 18:18

The phrase to "smite him with the tongue" is better rendered "smite him on the tongue." In some countries in the Middle East, even to this day, the punishment for lying is administered "by smiting the sinner on the mouth with a strong piece of leather like the sole of a shoe." The phrase appears as a condemnation, by the wicked of his day, toward Jeremiah. It is contained in this verse, "Then said they, Come, and let us devise devices against Jeremiah; for the law shall not perish from the priest, nor counsel from the wise, nor the word from the prophet. Come, and let us **smite him with the tongue**, and let us not give heed to any of his words" (Jeremiah 18:18; emphasis added). If Jeremiah's enemies did not intend to strike him with a strong piece of leather, they may have intended to punish him with authoritative words. If so, it would be like being beaten down verbally. Today one might say that he "got a real tongue lashing," or that someone surely "has a sharp tongue."

"move mountains" Matthew 17:20

Jesus taught those who believed in his mission the need for and the power of faith. He gave assurance that barriers and things that seemingly stand in our way can be overcome or removed. "And Jesus said unto them, Because of your unbelief: for verily I say unto you, If ye have faith as a grain of mustard seed, ye shall say unto this mountain, Remove hence to yonder place; and it shall remove; and nothing shall be impossible unto you" (Matthew 17:20).

This is perfect metaphorical hyperbole. Such expressions never caused misunderstanding because the people knew what he was saying applied to their lives and not to the physical features of the earth. It is the same today. President Gordon B. Hinckley spoke in general conference and titled his talk, "The Faith to Move Mountains." He spoke of the prayers of the Saints that had brought about the miracle and improvement of his own health, as he and other Church leaders tried to overcome seemingly impossible tasks that faced the growing Church.[1] Mountains facing us can be overcome. Rivers can be crossed, and chasms can be traversed. These are manners of speech that metaphorically empower our language.

Notes

1. Gordon B. Hinckley, "The Faith to Move Mountains," *Ensign*, Nov. 2006, 82.

IDIOMS MISUNDERSTOOD BECAUSE TRANSLATION WAS MADE OUT OF CONTEXT

"camel to go through the eye of a needle" Matthew 19:24

This is a very troublesome verse and is covered by almost every interpreter of scriptural texts. This saying results from a young man coming to the Savior and asking what he should do to enter into the kingdom of God. Jesus told him to sell all that he had and give it to the poor. This caused the rich young man to go away sorrowing. The verses that follow are:

> 23 Then said Jesus unto his disciples, Verily I say unto you, That a rich man shall hardly enter into the kingdom of heaven.
>
> 24 And again I say unto you, It is easier for a **camel to go through the eye of a needle**, than for a rich man to enter into the kingdom of God.
>
> 25 When his disciples heard it, they were exceedingly amazed,

saying, Who then can be saved?

26 But Jesus beheld them, and said unto them, With men this is impossible; but with God all things are possible. (Matthew 19:23–26; emphasis added)

In order to make a literal translation sensible, many follow the interpretation of Theophylact, Archbishop of Achrida in Bulgaria. In the eleventh century, he wrote that there was a gate in the walls of Jerusalem. He taught this even though he had never visited the city of Jerusalem. Additionally, the walls of Jerusalem had been torn down by conquerors twice before his time. Today, notable historians say that there never was such a gate and his idea of needing to unload the camels of their burdens before they could go through such a gate is totally false. So what is the meaning of this difficult teaching of the Savior? The contextual idea of the verse is that having riches makes entering the kingdom of God either difficult or impossible is obvious. However, which is it?

Robert Bradshaw sides with the interpretation made by Gordon D. Fee and Douglas Stuart. Fee and Stuart said, "After all, it is impossible for a camel to go through the eye of a needle, and that was precisely Jesus' point. It is impossible for one who trusts in riches to enter the kingdom. It takes a miracle for a rich person to get saved, which is quite the point of what follows 'All things are possible with God' "[1]

George M. Lamsa interpreted what Jesus said as follows:

The Aramaic word *gamla* means camel, a large rope, and a beam. The meaning of the word is determined by its context. If the word *riding* or *burden* occurs then gamla means a camel, but when the eye of a needle is mentioned gamla more correctly means a rope. There is no connection anywhere in Aramaic speech or literature between camel and needle, but there is a definite connection between rope and needle. Eastern women when purchasing thread often say, "It is a rope. I cannot use it," which means it is too thick. Then again, there are ropes in every Eastern home, used to tie up burdens on the backs of men and of animals. When not used, the rope is hung on the wall or laid in a corner of the house.[2]

All these writers agree that one who trusts in riches cannot enter God's kingdom. However, just because a person has riches, does not mean that he trusts in those same possessions. Lamsa leaves open the possibility for those having riches to obtain the kingdom of heaven, by indicating that there are both small and large needles, and with care a large thread or rope could possibly be used. Such large needles could have been those which they used to mend their fishing nets or to fasten together hides of animals. However, if we are left with uncertainty, verse 25 indicates we are not alone, for even Jesus' disciples had remaining questions. Remember, they asked, "Who then can be saved?" (Matthew 19:25).

"fed by ravens" 1 Kings 17:4

Elijah is told by the Lord to go to a spring just outside Jericho where he can have water during the time of drought and famine. For food, the King James text reads that he will be fed by ravens. "And it shall be, that thou shalt drink of the brook; and I have commanded the **ravens** to feed thee there" (1 Kings 17:4; emphasis added). The word translated into English as *ravens* was a Hebrew and Aramaic word which had multiple uses. Besides referring to a certain bird, it also meant "black" or "dark." Since ravens were considered unclean under the Mosaic Law, and also because they were scavengers, it seems unlikely that they would have been acceptable to provide food for Elijah in quality as well as quantity. A better translation would be that Elijah was fed by nomads who were Arabs and who were identified by their dark skin or appearance. There are some who want to hold onto the translation as being literal. However, this does not answer the question why a woman is sometimes referred to as a "raven" or a dark-haired beauty. Such a designation and use of the word *raven* is never associated with the fowl who is always looking for a meal. But to be a raven is generally considered a compliment to a black-haired woman. A more enlightened position to take regarding Elijah being fed is that he was fed by cousins, other descendants of Abraham, against whom the famine was not prophesied.

"wise as serpents, and harmless as doves" Matthew 10:16

The harmlessness of doves is easy to understand, for the dove is considered a symbol of peace. But to be wise as serpents is another matter. Today, it is said by many that we should "be wise as serpents, and harmless as doves." Some say it not knowing that its origin is from the Bible. Wise as serpents leaves more to be imagined or interpreted. However, such imagining is unnecessary if the change Joseph Smith made to the text is used. He changed the text to read, "Be . . . wise servants" rather than wise as serpents. The full statement of the Savior reads in JST Matthew 10:16, "be ye therefore wise servants, and as harmless as doves." The power of this different look is felt by knowing that the Savior was, at that time, giving instructions to the Twelve wherein he taught them that they were to be servants to the believers. They needed to be wise more than cunning.

Notwithstanding the change made by Joseph Smith to Matthew's account, we find the following instructions to Joseph and others who set themselves on a serious mission to Salem, Massachusetts in 1836: "Therefore, be ye as **wise as serpents** and yet without sin; and I will order all things for your good, as fast as ye are able to receive them. Amen" (D&C 111:11; emphasis added).

This revelation was recorded by a scribe or clerk for Joseph Smith. Following the first publication of the "Book of Commandment," Joseph made corrections to several clerical errors. Those changes he made were never included in future editions of "The Doctrine and Covenants of the Church of Christ," which were published in England and have since followed the uncorrected first printing. Likely this is one of those changes he intended to harmonize with his change in the account of Matthew. For an entire summary of this situation, consider the explanation given for the idiom "they are to be used sparingly."

"strait is the gate," "a straight and narrow path" Matthew 7:14

Since many words English are homonyms, the mind interprets the word by sound and attaches it to a meaning because of the familiar sound of the word, but misses the correct meaning. Such is the case with "straight" and "strait." Jesus said, "Because **strait** is the gate, and narrow is the way, which leadeth unto life, and few there be that find it" (Matthew 7:14; emphasis added). But John the Baptist taught regarding the Messiah, "For this is he that was spoken of by the prophet Esaias, saying, The voice of one crying in the wilderness, Prepare ye the way of the Lord, make his paths **straight**" (Matthew 3:3; emphasis added).

This problem evidently was the reason for several changes in the 1979 edition of the Book of Mormon. Up until that time verses such as 1 Nephi 8:20 read, "And I also beheld a **straight and narrow path**, which came along by the rod of iron, even to the tree by which I stood;

and it also led by the head of the fountain, unto a large and spacious field, as if it had been a world." However, in the new edition, many uses of the word *straight* were changed. The verse just cited was changed to read "**strait and narrow path.**"

Both of these phrases are idioms. They both indicate the manner by which we should live and obey. *Straight* means that we should not deviate. Today it could be illustrated by saying that "he's sure a straight arrow of a guy." Or one may say, "Are you being straight with me?"

Strait means to be restrained or controlled. It indicates that you don't have allowance. Everyone has a bit of fear that they may someday be placed into a strait jacket and be institutionalized. Such a jacket restricts the movements of your arms and limits destructive actions to yourself as well as to others. In addition, a strait is a narrow passage which must be carefully navigated to avoid perilous unseen dangers. An example would be the Straits of Magellan.

It seemed that few readers of the Book of Mormon noticed or realized the changes from "straight" to "strait" when they were made. But great thought and deliberation were applied to whether the changes reflected what had been verbally translated from the plates. Not every "straight was changed to "strait." Examples of other verses that were changed are 2 Nephi 31:18–19. Some readers seemed to feel that it made little or no difference. However, this is similar to how some lovers don't notice certain inferences that are spoken. And sometimes words poorly or incorrectly used could get you a "cold shoulder" or a place "in the dog house."

"strain at a gnat, and swallow a camel" Matthew 23:24

How do you do that? Strain at a gnat? Yes, it seems about as preposterous as swallowing a camel. However, this idiom makes much more sense if we realize that this is a poor translation of what was said by the Savior. Most likely he made a comparison (metaphor) of straining a small thing, such as a gnat, out of their milk, and consuming something the size of the whole camel (hyperbole). Remember, he was talking to the leaders who accused him of breaking the Law of Moses in trivial ways. At the same time, they offended the whole law by not accepting Jesus' divinity. So he said, "Ye blind guides, which strain at a gnat, and swallow a camel" (Matthew 23:24). Note the clarity if the verse were to read, "Ye blind guides, which strain **out** a gnat, and swallow a camel."

Daniel H. Ludlow made this assessment:

> The KJV is a relatively conservative translation. This is generally
> a strength, although at times it produces obscure renderings. More-
> over, some of its diction is now archaic and ungrammatical in current
> usage, and it is not consistent in the spelling of names in the Old and
> New Testaments (for example, Isaiah/Esaias and Elijah/Elias). Identi-
> cal words in the synoptic Gospels are sometimes translated differently,
> and some misprints were never corrected, (for instance, in Matt. 23:24,
> 'strain at a gnat' should have been rendered 'strain out a gnat').[3]

Considering even further, this may be another of those instances
wherein the Savior used a pun or a play on words. He could have chosen
other objects rather than a gnat and a camel. Such a pun would not
have been obvious in English, or even Greek. He would have said it
in Aramaic. He may have used like sounding words which suggested
multiple meanings. He used the words *galma* and *gamla*. The first, in
Aramaic, means "gnat," and the second, "camel." We use little couplet
phrases today to make points, such as "might makes right," "green as
grass," and "be there or be square." For certain, we know that Jesus'
meaning was clear and forceful, probably serious, but flavored with a
bit of humor, so it would not have been unusual for him to use a play
on words like this one.

"hate his father and mother" Luke 14:26

Since Jesus taught us to love one another and not to hate, Luke's
statement seems very out of context or poorly translated. Luke recorded,
"And there went great multitudes with him: and he turned, and said
unto them, If any man come to me, and hate not his father, and mother,
and wife, and children, and brethren, and sisters, yea, and his own life
also, he cannot be my disciple" (Luke 14:25–26). The word *hate* is a
poor choice of translation. The word Luke recorded, whether accurately
reported by him or not, would be better translated as "put aside" rather
than *hate*. This would harmonize with the first and greatest commandment, "And thou shalt love the Lord thy God with all thy heart, and
with all thy soul, and with all thy mind, and with all thy strength: this
is the first commandment" (Mark 12:30), as well as the advice given to
the rich young ruler (see Matthew 19:16–22).

Joseph Smith seemed to have the essence of the message, even
though he left the word *hate* in the verse, he clarified it with "or in

other words." The Joseph Smith Translation reads, "If any man come to me, and hate not his father, and mother, and wife, and children, and brethren, and sisters, or husband, yea and his own life also; or in other words, **is afraid to lay down his life for my sake,** cannot be my disciple" (JST Luke 14:26; emphasis added).

Notes

1. Robert I. Bradshaw, *Figures of Speech*, http://www. biblicalstudies.org.uk/article_idioms.html
2. George M. Lamsa, *Gospel Light* (San Francisco: Holman, 1939), 115.
3. Daniel H. Ludlow, *Encyclopedia of Momonism* (New York: Macmillan, 1992), 109.

IDIOMS
REGARDING
THE BODY

When Jacob, or Israel, gave blessings to each of his sons, he used some phrases which are seldom used today; therefore, we often do not understand their meanings. The blessing to Judah is filled with idioms. Some of these idioms are highlighted and discussed. His blessing reads:

> 8 Judah, thou art he whom thy brethren shall praise: **thy hand shall be in the neck of thine enemies**; thy father's children shall bow down before thee.
>
> 9 Judah is a lion's whelp: from the prey, my son, thou art gone up: he stooped down, he couched as a lion, and as an old lion; who shall rouse him up?
>
> 10 The **sceptre shall not depart from Judah**, nor a lawgiver from between his feet, until Shiloh come; and unto him shall the gathering of the people be.
>
> 11 Binding his foal unto the vine, and his ass's colt unto the choice vine; **he washed his garments in wine**, and his **clothes in the blood of grapes**:
>
> 12 His **eyes shall be red with wine**, and his **teeth white with milk** (Genesis 49:8–12; emphasis added).

"thy hand shall be in the neck of thine enemies"
Prophetically, Jacob proclaimed that his son Judah would be

27

blessed while living among others. Jacob said in his father-to-son bless-ing, "Thy hand shall be in the neck of thine enemies" (Genesis 49:8). This idiom indicated that Judah and his descendants would have power over their enemies. If you have your hand (a symbol for action) in the neck (a symbol for vulnerability) of your enemies, that is a strong mes-sage that you will be an incontrovertible power over your adversaries. All of Jacob's children bowed down to David and Solomon, who were from the tribe of Judah. Then there came the division of the rest of the tribes under Jeroboam as they opposed the leadership of Rehoboam, son of Solomon who reigned over the tribe of Judah. Assyria captured the tribes within Israel, and Judah alone remained intact for more than one hundred years before being taken into bondage. And since then, Judah has made a significant return to Palestine while the other tribes remain scattered and unorganized.

After being in captivity for centuries, the Jews have had unusual power regarding wealth, science, and the arts. Since 1957, Jews have truly had their hand in the neck of their avowed enemies, who are much larger and supported by other neighboring states. This all has taken place while the tiny state of Israel wields enormous influence in the world community as well as among its self-proclaimed enemies, who plan and work toward Israel's extermination. The descendants of Judah have been disobedient to God on many occasions and have suffered almost unimaginable bondage and atrocities. They, however, have come off as conquerors and, at present, are fulfilling the prophetic idiom pronounced by Jacob upon his son Judah. They truly have their hand in the neck of their enemies.

"the sceptre shall not depart from Judah"

The scepter was held by the king, both literally and figuratively. When this promise was made to Judah in his blessing, Jacob, Judah was promised that his posterity would be the line of kings that would rule. It started with David and Solomon and continued through cap-tivity, though in lineage and title only, until the birth of Jesus, who is king forever. Jesus was born as a Jew or descendant of Judah and both Matthew and Luke give his basic lineage. They gave this lineage to indicate that Jesus, of whom they were testifying, was king of the Jews and all Israel, and also the ruler of heaven and earth. The promise that prophesied this blessing to Judah reads as follows: "**The sceptre shall**

not depart from Judah, nor a lawgiver from **between his feet,** until Shiloh come; and unto him shall the gathering of the people be" (Genesis 49:10; emphasis added).

In addition to the statement that the sceptre would always be in the tribe of Judah, another idiom follows it in the promise. It is "between his feet." This is another euphemism meaning his literal offspring, conceived because of sexual actions taking place between the feet (and legs), thus indicating actual descendants.

"washed his garments in wine, and his clothes in the blood of grapes"

Jacob prophesied that Judah would "[**wash**] **his garment in wine**" (Genesis 49:11). This was to indicate that he would be the possessor of many vineyards. This is furthered by the phrase that he also would wash "**his clothes in the blood of grapes.**" The blood of grapes was their juice and if you had wine, it was an indication of wealth. To say that you had enough of it so you could wash your garments in wine, as opposed to using water, is hyperbole to the fullest. Forget about the staining of garments by the wine. Today, we use similar hyperbole by saying such things as "he throws money around like it's going out of style," or "he's got deep pockets," or "he rolls his cigars with 100 dollar bills." These idioms indicate wealth in abundance. They are examples of hyperbole. These idioms are things that you would literally not do, but just the fact that you could do it is the message. None of these idioms are factual, but they paint a picture of abundance. That was the blessing given to Judah. Are Jews considered to be wealthy? Just check out the wealth and power of people whose surnames are conclusively Jewish. An example would be names which end with "ein," such as Klein, Bernstein, Einstein, and Stein. Do these names "ring any bells"?

"his eyes shall be red with wine"

Jacob also foretold of Judah that "**his eyes shall be red with wine**" (Genesis 49:12), indicating that his descendants would drink in abundance from their vineyards.

"his teeth white with milk"

Last of all Judah would have "**his teeth white with milk**" (Genesis 49:12). This idiom foretold that he would have abundant flocks of sheep and goats. Other idioms use this same hyperbole and show abundance and prosperity or the lack thereof:

- "[winepresses] shall overflow with wine and oil" (Joel 2:24)

- "hills shall flow with milk" (Joel 3:18)
- "drink wine in bowls" (Amos 6:6), rather than from cups
- "shall not see the rivers, the floods, the brooks of honey and butter"—the lot of the wicked (Job 20:17)

These idioms are very logical and not unlike such idioms used today, such as, "He's got money to burn"; "He's filthy rich"; "He was born with a silver spoon in his mouth"; He can make a silk purse out of a sow's ear;" and "Everything he touches turns to gold."

"dip his foot in oil"

Moses likewise blessed the descendants of Jacob's sons prior to their entering the promised land. Asher was blessed as follows: "And of Asher he said, Let Asher be blessed with children; let him be acceptable to his brethren, and let him **dip his foot in oil**" (Deuteronomy 33:24; emphasis added). This idiom should indicate to us that his people would become prosperous. Oil is a symbol of prosperity, and he wouldn't just look at the oil, nor touch it, but dip his foot in oil. That's like saying "He's got his finger in everyone's business," "He's got his hand in the till," or "How did you get your foot in the door?"

"cleanness of teeth"

During the apostate times wherein Amos was not able to get his people to return to God in obedience and righteousness, the Lord said to him, "And I also have given you **cleanness of teeth** in all your cities, and want of bread in all your places: yet have ye not returned unto me, saith the Lord" (Amos 4:6; emphasis added). Even though Amos had to suffer through these conditions with his people, it seems that God is telling Amos that he had blessed them with "cleanness of teeth." This idiom should be identified as a metaphor, telling of times of famine. Today, we try to indicate hard times with "we're going to have to tighten our belts a lot before we get through this."

"shall dwell between his shoulders"

Between one's shoulders are the heart and other organs that are the fountain of feelings. Benjamin's tribe or descendants are blessed or promised that they would have a special place amongst the other tribes. Remember, Benjamin was the youngest of the sons of Jacob or Israel. Also remember that his mother, Rachel, Jacob's first love, died in the process of giving birth to Benjamin. Moses declares as one of his last performances, "And of Benjamin he said, The beloved of the Lord shall dwell in safety by him; and the Lord shall cover him all the day long, and he **shall dwell between his shoulders**" (Deuteronomy 33:12; emphasis added). The tribe of Benjamin was usually at peace with the other tribes, and many Benjaminites were absorbed into the Kingdom of Judah and thus, in part, they escaped Assyrian captivity.

"cover his feet"

This idiom is obscured from Western readers because men of Western culture have not worn robes and girdles. For centuries, Western men have worn pants or trousers. They have to imagine what clothing would do if you were wearing a robe and you did not have a toilet upon which to seat yourself when you relieved your bowels. Not only would your skirt or robe cover your feet as you squatted, but it would provide some privacy right on the spot. Understanding this idiom sheds enlightenment to what is happening in the following verses:

- "When he was gone out, his servants came; and when they saw that, behold, the doors of the parlour were locked, they said, Surely **he covereth his feet** in his summer chamber" (Judges 3:24; emphasis added).
- "And he came to the sheepcotes by the way, where was a cave; and Saul went in to **cover his feet**: and David and his men remained in the sides of the cave" (1 Samuel 24:3; emphasis added).

This is why David was able to take advantage of Saul. The king left all his guards and went by himself to relieve himself. David watched from a distance and went to the spot where Saul had removed the burden of his armor, canteen, and weapons, so as to take care of his natural needs.

"he goeth out unto the water"

Without sewer facilities, a people residing in the same location would find a river to be a great benefit. Not only would a stream be your supply of potable water, but it would carry away your waste. Such was the case regarding the Nile River and the Pharaoh of Egypt. Moses and Aaron wanted to have an audience with the Pharaoh and he was not making himself available to them. Therefore, the Lord told Moses and Aaron how to speak to the Pharaoh when none of his court would be with him. The Lord said, "Get thee unto Pharaoh in the morning; lo, he **goeth out unto the water**; and thou shalt stand by the river's brink against he come" (Exodus 7:15; emphasis added). So they found the spot where the Pharaoh went in the mornings to urinate and relieve himself into the river and waited until he came there by himself. There they were able to deliver their message. Today we still have many idioms for this natural compulsion, none of which need to be written here.

"gathered up his feet"

Drawing one's feet up and bending the knees into a fetal position is a natural action when one is not feeling well or is in pain. Both of these conditions generally exist preceding death. So this idiom is a descriptive way of saying that the person died. "And when Jacob had made an end of commanding his sons, he **gathered up his feet** into the bed, and yielded up the ghost, and was gathered unto his people" (Genesis 49:33; emphasis added). Today, we use many such idioms to indicate death. We say, "He took his last breath." We also say that "he crossed over," or "passed on." We might even say that "he bought the farm," or "was taken home."

"became as a stone"

Since a stone never moves or changes on its own, it is such a natural symbol for being dead. Notice the account during David's time, "But it came to pass in the morning, when the wine was gone out of Nabal, and his wife had told him these things, that his heart died within him, and **he became as a stone**" (1 Samuel 25:37; emphasis added). Surely Nabal became rigid upon death, but the idiom indicates that he transitioned from life to death quickly to become like a stone. A modern equivalent would be "he's stone dead." It could be concluded that he had a heart attack or a stroke.

"did eat grass as oxen"

When King Nebuchadnezzar walked in his palace with real pride because of his conquering conquests, God spoke to him and told him that things would change. He was told that certain things would happen until finally he would turn his eyes to the most high God. Prominent, within many other figurative expressions in the story, is the phrase "eat grass as oxen." If you know that this idiom is one that indicates losing one's mind, the change with the king is much more understandable. Read it all:

30 The king spake, and said, Is not this great Babylon, that I have built for the house of the kingdom by the might of my power, and for the honour of my majesty?

31 While the word was in the king's mouth, there fell a voice from heaven, saying, O king Nebuchadnezzar, to thee it is spoken; The kingdom is departed from thee.

32 And they shall drive thee from men, and thy dwelling shall be with the beasts of the field: they shall make thee to **eat grass as oxen**, and seven times shall pass over thee, until thou know that the most High ruleth in the kingdom of men, and giveth it to whomsoever he will.

33 The same hour was the thing fulfilled upon Nebuchadnezzar: and he was driven from men, and **did eat grass as oxen**, and his body was wet with the dew of heaven, till his hairs were grown like eagles' feathers, and his nails like birds' claws.

34 And at the end of the days I Nebuchadnezzar lifted up mine eyes unto heaven, **and mine understanding returned unto me**, and I blessed the most High, and I praised and honoured him that liveth for ever, whose dominion is an everlasting dominion, and his kingdom is from generation to generation:

35 And all the inhabitants of the earth are reputed as nothing: and he doeth according to his will in the army of heaven, and among the inhabitants of the earth: and none can stay his hand, or say unto him, What doest thou?

36 At the same time my reason returned unto me; and for the glory of my kingdom, mine honour and brightness returned unto me; and my counsellors and my Lords sought unto me; and I was established in my kingdom, and excellent majesty was added unto me.

37 Now I Nebuchadnezzar praise and extol and honour the King of heaven, all whose works are truth, and his ways judgment: and those that walk in pride he is able to abase (Daniel 4:30–37; emphasis added).

"put his hand upon thine eyes"

Jacob was worried about believing his other sons when they told him that his son Joseph was alive (see Genesis 45:25–28). Jacob's sons had lied to him previously regarding their brother Joseph, and Jacob also feared to go with them in his old age to Egypt where Joseph was. The idiom describes death because eyes of the deceased are often partially or completely open. Traditionally, and out of kindness, a relative or an attendant who cares, will softly put their hand over the face as they close the eyelids. Notice the words God used to assure Jacob: "I will go down with thee into Egypt; and I will also surely bring thee up again: and Joseph shall **put his hand upon thine eyes**" (Genesis 46:4; emphasis added). What a reassuring promise to Jacob. Joseph would be the one to "put his hand upon [his] eyes."

"my skin"

Proper punctuation in the King James text would help us identify this idiom. However, the translators or scribes didn't give us that clarity. Therefore, modern readers simply think that Job is referring to skin worms which would consume his mortal body. Yes, maybe worms would destroy his body, but not skin worms. The idiom "my skin" or simply "skin," is a phrase regarding life (e.g. "He tried to save his own skin.") Today, golfers play a game called skins. It has a different set of rules. They play until one of them wins the hole and the other players are dead. This player then gets the skin or life. So with this thought of "my skin" referring to one's life, read the powerful testimony of Job. However, as you read his words, make certain that you mentally place a comma and generate an appropriate pause, right after the word *skin*. Notice the wonderful transformation that occurs to his declaration as you do so. "And though after my skin[,] worms destroy this body, yet in my flesh shall I see God" (Job 19:26). Job was testifying that after his life (skin), worms would destroy his flesh, and yet because of the promised Resurrection, he would be resurrected, and he would one day be in his flesh again and see God.

"men's hearts shall fail them"

More than any other time in history, heart surgical procedures are administered in great numbers. Some have said in jest, but some seriously, that this is a sign that the Lord's return is near. They base their conclusion upon the following, "And in that day shall be heard of wars and rumors of wars, and the whole earth shall be in commotion, and **men's hearts shall fail them**, and they shall say that Christ delayeth his coming until the end of the earth" (D&C 45:26; emphasis added).

It is helpful to know that God and his prophets have made reference to the "heart" to indicate conditions that go far beyond the physical. Whenever the word *heart* is used, the things that should come to one's mind should be in the categories of feelings and determination, sympathy and courage. Remember what the Lord said to Oliver Cowdery through Joseph regarding revelation? The Lord said, "Yea, behold, I will tell you **in your mind and in your heart**, by the Holy Ghost, which shall come upon you and which shall **dwell in your heart**" (D&C 8:2; emphasis added).

Being aware of how the Lord uses the word *heart* when he speaks or directs should point us to a greater danger, one that is not centered on that one organ of the body. God also stated, "And all things shall be in commotion; and surely, **men's hearts shall fail them**; for fear shall come upon all people" (D&C 88:91; emphasis added). I hope we can understand the concerns properly which God expresses. They are less regarding the physical and more of the spiritual. They speak less of life and death and more of hearing and obeying.

The best rule to follow while reading scripture that contains the word *heart* or *hearts*, would be to substitute the word *feeling* or *feelings* in their place. An oft-quoted verse that uses the word *heart* reads, "Trust in the Lord with all thine **heart** [substitute **feelings**]; and lean not unto thine own understanding. In all thy ways acknowledge him, and he shall direct thy paths" (Proverbs 3:5–6; emphasis added).

Applying the same principle to "men's hearts shall fail them" as quoted above, is it not true? Are not men's feelings failing them today? We see senseless death, war, waste, and pollution. We see men acting like animals rather than children of God. Yes, men's feelings are failing them!

"put thy hand under my thigh"

The action of putting "thy hand under my thigh," is a bit irregular for us today. It is used regarding two episodes recorded in Genesis.

1 And Abraham was old, and well stricken in age: and the Lord had blessed Abraham in all things.

2 And Abraham said unto his eldest servant of his house, that ruled over all that he had, Put, I pray thee, **thy hand under my thigh**:

3 And I will make thee swear by the Lord, the God of heaven, and the God of the earth, that thou shalt not take a wife unto my son of the daughters of the Canaanites, among whom I dwell:

4 But thou shalt go unto my country, and to my kindred, and take a wife unto my son Isaac.

5 And the servant said unto him, Peradventure the woman will not be willing to follow me unto this land: must I needs bring thy son again unto the land from whence thou camest?

6 And Abraham said unto him, Beware thou that thou bring not my son thither again.

7 The Lord God of heaven, which took me from my father's house, and from the land of my kindred, and which spake unto me, and that sware unto me, saying, Unto thy seed will I give this land; he shall send his angel before thee, and thou shalt take a wife unto my son from thence.

8 And if the woman will not be willing to follow thee, then thou shalt be clear from this my oath: only bring not my son thither again.

9 And the servant **put his hand under the thigh** of Abraham his master, and sware to him concerning that matter" (Genesis 24:1–9; emphasis added).

29 And the time drew nigh that Israel must die: and he called his son Joseph, and said unto him, If now I have found grace in thy sight, put, I pray thee, **thy hand under my thigh**, and deal kindly and truly with me; bury me not, I pray thee, in Egypt:

30 But I will lie with my fathers, and thou shalt carry me out of Egypt, and bury me in their buryingplace. And he said, I will do as thou hast said.

31 And he said, Swear unto me. And he sware unto him. And Israel bowed himself upon the bed's head (Genesis 47:29–31; emphasis added).

The word *testicle* in the dictionary originates from the Latin word "testis" or witness. The word *testicle* is associated with many courtroom related words: *testify*, *testament*, and the French word *temoin*, which means witness. According to Dr. Bob Fisher, a professor of linguistics at the University of Toronto, testicles played an important part in ancient courtrooms. Today we swear on a Bible. In ancient days, a man had to grab his own testicles or those of his friend in order to validate his testimony. He would let go only when he'd finished testifying. In those patriarchal times, women did not make an appearance in the courtroom.

Clearly this was a literal action "put thy hand under my thigh"; however, it is also another euphemism. The action was much more than simply a hand under the thigh. It was just like saying "I put my foot in my mouth," "my arm to the square," or "my hand over my heart." The physical action may or may not actually occur, but the metaphorical message of the idiom is there to be understood.

Joseph Smith changed the word *thigh* to *hand* in his translation. His text reads, "And Abraham said unto his eldest servant of his house, that ruled over all that he had; Put forth I pray thee thy hand under my **hand**" (JST Genesis 24:2; emphasis added). His change may not have been to substitute Abraham's hand for his own thigh. Abraham may well have been instructing his servant to put his hand under Abraham's thigh along with Abraham's own hand. There may be no conflict at all between Joseph Smith's translation and the original but only clarification.

As Jacob or Israel's life was closing, he called Joseph his son to him. He instructed Joseph to put his hand under his thigh and promise him that he would not bury him in Egypt but take his body back to Canaan, the land of his inheritance. Joseph Smith does not change this verse the same as the previously cited reference. Reasons for changing or not changing either could be debated. However, the roots and meaning of the word *testicle* and its corresponding uses regarding promises applies in all instances.

"as the Lord liveth"

This idiom leads us to what the Savior did himself. Knowing that he has all power, he cannot forswear! So he can swear by living things. And he does!

When instructing and promising the three witnesses of the Book of Mormon plates, the Lord told them they would be able to see the breastplate, the plates, and the Urim and Thummim. But then he swore to them that the record Joseph had translated was true. Notice the words he uses, "And he has translated the book, even that part which I have commanded him, and **as your Lord and your God liveth it is true** (D&C 17:6; emphasis added).

This idiomatic phrase was used by Nephi to Zoram when he brought the plates to Nephi, thinking that he was Laban. Something must have calmed Zoram and kept him from escaping from Nephi at some point and returning to Jerusalem. It must have been Nephi's sure promise. "And it came to pass that I spake with him, that if he would hearken unto my words, **as the Lord liveth**, and as I live, even so that if he would hearken unto our words, we would spare his life" (1 Nephi 4:32; emphasis added).

This idiomatic phrase appears twenty-eight times in the Bible, sixteen times in the Book of Mormon, and two times in the Doctrine and Covenants. Of course the Lord lives! But this idiom says more than that great truth. It says that since the Lord lives, then many more things are also true. Men have forsworn themselves and sworn by God, hell, and many things in between. All they have done is shown they do not understand who God really is as well as their lack of the relationship they are to have with him. When we swear by something living, we make an oath. Many who do not honor the name of God do not understand the thing they unknowingly do when they swear or curse. There are many other prevarications that include this pattern established by the Lord of swearing by something that is living. However, it is very interesting to note examples in scripture such as D&C 17:6 of the Lord doing that very thing. Nephi's promise to Zoram is another example of a solemn oath. When the Lord makes an oath, he cannot break it.

IDIOMS
REGARDING
CUSTOMS AND
TRADITIONS

"took up our carriages"

If you heard the idiom, "I got it straight from the horse's mouth," and didn't understand what it meant, you would be clueless as to what really took place. The same is true in the following verses regarding carriages or one's carriage. Readers tend to identify a carriage as a vehicle used for travel. However, carriages were not the thing upon which they rode, but the possessions that they carried. Read the following verses with this in mind and notice the difference this change makes in each event:

- And after those days we **took up our carriages**, and went up to Jerusalem. (Acts 21:15; emphasis added)
- He is come to Aiath, he is passed to Migron; at Michmash he hath **laid up his carriages**. (Isaiah 10:28; emphasis added)
- So they turned and departed, and put the little ones and the cattle **and the carriage** before them. (Judges 18:21; emphasis added)
- And David **left his carriage** in the hand of the keeper of the **carriage**, and ran into the army, and came and saluted his brethren. (1 Samuel 17:22; emphasis added)

"and all the furniture"

Because of the poor translation of certain words, some passages in scripture lack clarity. One verse that conjures up unusual questions, tells of the "camel's furniture." Knowing that the word *furniture* should read "furnishings" or "supplies" would help the story greatly. The verse, without the surrounding story, reads, "Now Rachel had taken the images, and put them in the **camel's furniture**, and sat upon them. And Laban searched all the tent, but found [them] not" (Genesis 31:34; emphasis added). Some will be prone to think of some sort of framework or saddle as the "camel's furniture." However, if we think of *furnishings* like blankets, harnesses, and other ornaments instead of *furniture* our mental picture of this event will be more accurate.

Another troublesome verse deals with the tabernacle. When you have read and determined the furnishings described to be in the tabernacle in the wilderness, you wonder if there were other furniture items that occupied the holy places. Consider this verse, "The tabernacle of the congregation, and the ark of the testimony, and the mercy seat that is thereupon, **and all the furniture** of the tabernacle" (Exodus 31:7; emphasis added). Some will equate furniture as meaning such articles as chairs and tables. However, if you know that the word *furniture* should be translated to mean furnishings, then your mental image could include ornaments, food, and oil, which all needed to be furnished. The word *furniture* is misleading and would be better written in our language as *furnishings*.

"speak to the rock"

Moses found himself faced with unexpected problems even after deliverance from Pharaoh's armies and the sea. The people cried for not only food, but water. Moses was instructed by the Lord to find water for the people. The Lord said, "Take the rod, and gather thou the assembly together, thou, and Aaron thy brother, and **speak ye unto the rock** before their eyes; and it shall give forth his water, and thou shalt bring forth to them water out of the rock: so thou shalt give the congregation and their beasts drink" (Numbers 20:8; emphasis added). "Speak ye unto the rock" is not literal. Rocks do not speak nor listen literally, but they do speak figuratively, just like the stock market talks to those who study it, or a rifle says that it is shooting to the right when you look at the paper target with its bull's-eye and circles. The wind and the rain talk to us, our bodies say that we have had enough exertion, and our automobile says that it isn't going to start.

To understand the context of the Lord's statement to Moses, it is interesting to know that when someone in Moses' day found or dug a well, they wanted it for their own use and not for others. They wanted to be assured that when they brought their flocks to water, there would be an ample supply, so they would attempt to hide it from other herdsmen. Their intent wasn't just to hide the water to have adequate supply, but to prevent other herdsman from grazing in the area. Another reason to hide or cover a well was to prevent it from being filled with foreign, potentially harmful material.

The most common manner to hide a well was to cover it with a stone. The way to discover a stone that covered a well was to use sound. The procedure was to strike the ground and rocks of an area with a staff or rod and listen for the sound that resulted. If a stone was covering a void, such as a hole or well, the resulting sound would be identified as contrary to the sound of the rocks lying on solid ground. Thus, the way they found hidden wells, previously dug by others, was to strike or "speak to the rock." The people Moses was leading had lived for centuries in the fertile valleys of the Nile River with its high water table. Obtaining water in the Nile required a small amount of digging to reach abundant water. But in the desert it was much different.

After leaving Egypt, Moses lived for years in the land of Midian with his father-in-law, Jethro, and herded flocks in the same kind of terrain in which his followers found themselves. While tending his flocks, Moses likely had to dig, hide, and find wells. The Lord told Moses to "speak ye unto the rock before their eyes," meaning Moses should teach the people the process of finding water in the desert. He told Moses to show the people how to obtain water by striking or "[speaking] unto the rock."

For Moses to say that he struck the rock and water came forth is very natural. Today, police officers "put the word out on the street" to see what they hear. To find out how someone will respond to an issue, we say, "I'll run that past a few people." While I traveled with a native Jewish guide in this very area of Sinai, the guide told of his army's need to find water during the pivotal six-day war in 1967 with Egypt. He clearly pointed out locations with features that indicated where water would likely be found. These soldiers located existing wells in this same manner. Upon finding water, what is reported? "We struck water!" Today it is not unusual for us to use idioms such as "We struck oil," or "I struck it rich!" Drillers say, "We struck a good flow of water at seventy-five feet." "Speaking to the rock" is as natural as "keeping your eye on the road " or "your ear to the ground."

"spit in the face"

Moses' sister Miriam joins Aaron in complaining against Moses during the trying times in the wilderness. In considering what should be done regarding her rebellion, the Lord directs Moses, "And the Lord said unto Moses, If her father had but **spit in her face**, should she not be ashamed seven days? let her be shut out from the camp seven days, and after that let her be received in again" (Numbers 12:14; emphasis added). The Lord was making reference to the action that was acceptable in the day. It was to literally spit in someone's face. It is still practiced in some cultures today as a rejection of business deals, proposals, and repudiations. It was a literal outward action showing strong rebuke. Jesus warned in the Sermon on the Mount regarding saying "Raca." He said, "But I say unto you, That whosoever is angry with his brother without a cause shall be in danger of the judgment: and whosoever shall say to his brother, Raca, shall be in danger of the council: but whosoever shall say, Thou fool, shall be in danger of hell fire" (Matthew 5:22). The word *raca* means "to spit." Therefore, both of these passages are speaking of the same practice. However, Jesus taught that we should control our urges to return evil for evil. He taught that we should speak strictly "yea" or "nay." Today one might figuratively say "I spit on what you did" as a strong rebuke. Or "he spit in my face" to mean he shamed me. That is the message God referenced in regards to Miriam and her father. Her father should have rebuked her, and then she likely would not have sided against Moses. This practice is like so many mandates. They are intended figuratively but practiced literally by those who are extreme or pious. Jesus attempted to correct some of these disciplines. The Pharisees especially had made many additions to what the Law of Moses prescribed. Jesus taught against these inflated rules, which were acceptable in the culture but would put the doer "in danger of hell fire."

"kick against the pricks"

To "kick against the pricks" is a phrase that describes the reaction of an animal, such as an ox's response to a goad or stick being thrust into its flanks by the handler to guide or direct the animal as it travels or pulls its load. If the animal does not like the prick or goad, then it kicks to shows its rebellion or reluctance to such prompting by its handler. Every cattle driver who has moved cattle in pens and chutes, or driven animals pulling a load, knows how to direct or motivate the animals by using a goad or prick. It is a common means to accomplish the task. To expect the animal to kick against such direction or motivation is natural. Many times the animal endangers itself by its own action of rebellious kicking.

So when the Lord appeared to Saul while he was on the road to Damascus, he used this idiom when speaking to him, to indicate that he had been prompting Saul to believe the story of the apostles who were testifying of the Messiah's crucifixion and resurrection. However, Saul was "kicking against the pricks" which, figuratively, the Lord had been using to direct him. Remember how the Lord said it to Saul: "And he said, Who art thou, Lord? And the Lord said, I am Jesus whom thou persecutest: it is hard for thee to **kick against the pricks**" (Acts 9:5; emphasis added). Saul was hurting others, but the greatest point the Lord was making that, like with the driven animals, Saul had the potential to hurt himself if he continued to rebel. Saul's story is recounted again later in Acts and the Lord uses the same idiom in that account: "And when we were all fallen to the earth, I heard a voice speaking unto me, and saying in the Hebrew tongue, Saul, Saul, why persecutest thou me? it is hard for thee to **kick against the pricks** (Acts 26:14; emphasis added).

The Lord also uses this idiom when speaking to the many that are called, but not chosen. He tells them that they set their hearts on the things of the world and do not learn the lesson that the powers of heaven are not controlled or handled other than by the principles of righteousness. And if one undertakes to control such powers in any degree of unrighteousness, he is left unto himself, to fight against God and to "kick against the pricks." The Lord said, "Behold, ere he is aware, he is left unto himself, to **kick against the pricks**, to persecute the saints, and to fight against God" (D&C 121:38; emphasis added).

"without purse or script"

The Lord has more than once directed his servants to go "without purse or script." We quickly understand that they are not to take money (purse), but what is meant by script? The answer to the question is that a script is a bag, in addition to a purse, that is used to carry things in addition to money or assets. It could be used to carry food or extra clothing and such. Notice how the Lord said it: "And he said unto them, When I sent you without purse, and scrip, and shoes, lacked ye any thing? And they said, Nothing. Then said he unto them, But now, he that hath a purse, let him take [it], and likewise [his] scrip: and he that hath no sword, let him sell his garment, and buy one" (Luke 22:35–36).

The next question regarding the Lord's instruction is: "Why did he give the instruction to not take purse or script?" (see Mark 6:8, Luke 10:4) The answer is that he did not want them to take possessions because they would be in danger of being robbed. But that is only part of the problem. The punishment for robbery was so severe that it was customary for thieves to kill their victims, thus silencing any witness to their treachery. Many have felt that God does not want his servants to take money and provision when in his service, because money and possessions are evil. It is more accurate to conclude that God is concerned for the safety of his servants. It is also possible that he wants them to be more dependent on his mercy and direction to have their physical needs met. Such instructions were not only given in New Testament times, but to servants in the Restoration period. Note the following:

- And thou shalt take no purse nor scrip, neither staves, neither two coats, for the church shall give unto thee in the very hour what thou needest for food and for raiment, and for shoes and for money, and for scrip. (D&C 24:18)
- For I suffered them not to have purse or scrip, neither two coats. (D&C 84:78)
- Therefore, let no man among you, for this commandment is unto all the faithful who are called of God in the church unto the ministry, from this hour take purse or scrip, that goeth forth to proclaim this gospel of the kingdom. (D&C 84:86)

"gird up your loins"

This idiom is an expression from the past even though it is used still today. It is an expression from the past because it was coined when men wore robes, skirts, cloaks, and girdles. A girdle was a sash or belt whose function was to hold the bulk of the garment from getting in the way while working. Not only did it hold the robe close to the waist and the loins, but the skirt of the garment would often get in the way of the legs when engaged in labors. Therefore the custom was to reach back through the legs and bring forward the back skirt of the robe between the legs and tuck it into the girdle which was around the waist. This action left the legs free and the robe pulled up against the groin and out of the way. It was an indication that a person was ready to do serious work. One of the labors that required such girding most was treading the wine press. The grapes were crushed by stomping or walking on the grapes with bare feet and skirts girdled. The girdle went around the waist and therefore over the loins as it held the person's clothing in place. Hence it was called the girding of the loins.

Like other idioms, there is much more meaning here than merely arranging your clothing. It suggests an attitude of readiness for labor. This message comes through in each of the verses in which the idiom appears. It is even the message in the moving hymn sung first by pioneers seeking a home far away in the West. Little wonder it moves so many to action when they sing, "gird up your loins; fresh courage take. Our God will never us forsake."[1]

The following is just a sampling of scriptural verses that contain the idiom. There are dozens from which to choose. There are as many in modern revelations, given in times when men did not wear robes and girdles, as there are in Bible times. It is figurative all the way.

- Wherefore, lift up your hearts and rejoice, and **gird up your loins**, and take upon you my whole armor, that ye may be able to withstand the evil day, having done all, that ye may be able to stand. (D&C 27:15; emphasis added).
- And their arm shall be my arm, and I will be their shield and their buckler; and I will **gird up their loins**, and they shall fight manfully for me; and their enemies shall be under their feet; and I will let fall the sword in their behalf, and by the fire of mine indignation will I preserve them (D&C 35:14; emphasis added).

- Wherefore, **gird up your loins** and be prepared. Behold, the kingdom is yours, and the enemy shall not overcome (D&C 38:9; emphasis added).
- Wherefore **gird up your loins** lest ye be found among the wicked (D&C 43:19; emphasis added).
- Therefore, **gird up thy loins** for the work. Let thy feet be shod also, for thou art chosen, and thy path lieth among the mountains, and among many nations. (D&C 112:7; emphasis added).
- Wherefore **gird up the loins** of your mind, be sober, and hope to the end for the grace that is to be brought unto you at the revelation of Jesus Christ (1 Peter 1:13; emphasis added).

"he hath sold us"

Such a desperate expression indicated a loss of freedom. It was an expression which indicated that a father or master had used for themselves a dowry promised to children. Beginning a household and obtaining herds or land was difficult without receiving a dowry from someone for whom you labored or from whom you were born. When Rachel and Leah considered leaving their brother and going with Jacob their husband, they gave one reason for not being loyal to their brother, who had acted in the place of their deceased father, as follows: "Are we not counted of him strangers? for he hath **sold us**, and hath quite devoured also our money" (Genesis 31:15; emphasis added).

"in the mouth of a fish"

Because of a poor translation into English, this idiom does not read well. The setting for the verse is when Jesus is challenged regarding the payment of tribute or taxes. Peter expresses concern to Jesus, and Jesus replies, "Notwithstanding, lest we should offend them, go thou to the sea, and cast an hook, and take up the fish that first cometh up; and when thou hast opened his mouth, thou shalt find a piece of money: that take, and give unto them for me and thee" (Matthew 17:27).

This instruction by Jesus seems so psychic. It would hold up well in a TV show today of "Last Psychic Standing." Being aware of idioms we say today is a pattern for how this idiom should have been translated. One might say, "I'll get twenty dollars out of that bicycle." Another might say, "I've got twenty-five hundred buried in that car." Neither of these sayings is meant to show that you can find money inside either vehicle just because the words *in* or *out* are used. You will find a shekel **in the mouth of a fish** means you will easily catch a fish and sell it for a shekel. An easterner will declare, "There are ten dollars in the horn of my ox." This means that my ox can be sold for ten dollars. "There is a dollar in each one of my goats" means each goat can be sold for a dollar.

Other expressions use the words *in* and *into* but are not meant to be literal. Today you might say: "I put twenty years of blood, sweat, and tears into that marriage." Or you could observe, "They put millions in that project and it went south."

The question regarding the shekel in the mouth of the fish is not about whether the Savior could do such a thing. Of course he could. He has all power. He is the creator of worlds. Guidance from God is more expected to take the form of promptings to make a certain purchase, to select a job or vocation, select a mate, and invest wisely, rather than to be directed to find money in the mouth of a fish.

"out of belly of hell cried I" "in a fish"

Jonah's story takes on a whole new dimension when you realize the idioms within his account have not been properly handled by translators. We know from his own words within chapter one that he has been called to bring the people of the great city Nivevah to repentance, but he becomes afraid and chooses to go elsewhere. Upon boarding his ship, he "went down into it, to go with them unto Tarshish from the presence of the Lord" (Jonah 1:3). Jonah is in trouble because he is going away "from the presence of the Lord"! How would we say it today? Possibly we might metaphorically say that "he is in hot water." We might also express that "he is up a creek without a paddle." We might use Paul's words that "we are tossed to and fro by every wind of doctrine," when we have been deceived. Jonah tells of the Lord sending great winds and a tempest in the sea (Jonah 1:4). We experience many messages from God when we disobey him.

Then Jonah tells, "Now the Lord had prepared a great fish to swallow up Jonah" (Jonah 1:17). The word *whale* is not used. But the key idiom of his day comes now into play. In his day if you were in trouble, you could tell others you were "**in a fish**," just like today one might say you are "in deep water," or "up to your neck in alligators."

"Then Jonah prayed unto the Lord his God out of the fish's belly, and said, I cried by reason of mine affliction unto the Lord, and he heard me; **out of the belly of hell** cried I, and thou heardest my voice" (Jonah 2:1–2; emphasis added). For those who read this literally, they picture Jonah praying while in the bowels of this great fish. In contrast, those who can identify the idiomatic language can picture Jonah praying while he is in this great turmoil or trouble.

Lehi was in great anguish when he saw his vision of the tree of life in the Book of Mormon. He partook of the fruit of the tree and found it to be desirous above all other fruit. Then he looked and saw his family. He beckoned to them to come to where he was. They came; however, Laman and Lemuel refused and would not come and partake of the fruit. (See 1 Nephi 8:10–18.) All of Lehi's experience is symbolic. The tree represents the love of God and partaking of the fruit represents partaking of the love of God. Sariah, Sam, and Nephi did not literally eat the fruit, but the reporting of the conditions in which Lehi found himself tell of actual events. Lehi used classic literary form to better describe what was really happening to him.

So it was with Jonah. He reported that he cried out to God in his troubles. He expressed that condition much the way a business owner tells his story by saying he is "going down with the ship" as his business fails. We understand what he is conveying by saying he is going down with the ship, and we also understand what he means if he says that someone "threw him a line." Such expressions tell much deeper feelings than saying, "The economy turned bad and I would have lost my business if someone had not paid me an old debt." Going down with the ship describes great hopelessness and despair. Seafarers know if you go down with a ship, likely your own life will be sucked under with the ship. They also know the surety of one rope. That is all that is needed to snatch a person from sure doom. That was the situation with Jonah. His is not simply a story of being swallowed by a fish, miraculous as it may seem. He tells of being swallowed by his disobedience and despair, but having his prayers heard by a merciful God, who saves him from destruction. Jonah is then given another chance to fulfill his calling. His expression of this is being expelled by the fish (his troubles) onto the shore.

The second idiom, "out of the belly of hell," harmonizes with being in a fish. That is where he is, not literally in a fish, but deep in anguish and distress (hell—even the belly or very center of hell) because of disobedience to God's word.

But Jonah finds faith and strength. He figuratively states, "When my soul fainted within me I remembered the Lord" (Jonah 2:7). And then he tells, in his metaphorical words, of his escape from his abandonment this way, "And the Lord spake unto the fish, and it vomited out Jonah upon the dry land" (Jonah 2:10).

If you choose to make Jonah's account literal, all of the figurative terminology must be considered literal. However, knowing the allegories, metaphors, and similes used throughout all scriptural texts should cause you to rejoice in the power and depictions rendered by a figurative interpretation. Once again, when we want to express our deepest emotions today, we likewise choose to use figurative language. I'd give my right arm if I only could help you see that. I'd give the sun, the moon, and the stars. I'd give my lucky rabbit's foot and every dime I own if it would help you see that this is why the Lord and his prophets use metaphors, similes, and parables. They don't just tell the situations, they cause us to feel and reflect.

"salt of the earth"

The Savior taught in the Sermon on the Mount that those who believed in his teachings which he had received from his Father in Heaven were of great worth. He said to them, "Ye are the **salt of the earth** " (Matthew 5:13). Salt was so valuable in ancient Rome that it was doled out to Caesar's soldiers as part of their pay. It was called "salarium," a word from which our term *salary* comes. In ancient Greece it was even common to exchange salt for slaves. When a slave didn't match his worth in labor, he was said to be "not worth his salt." This same idiom is spoken today when someone is not worth what they are being paid. Some idioms have made their way through centuries. Others fade and are forgotten after the conditions that spawned them change. Possibly the idea of salt was also used because of its ability to preserve foods. It is also associated with the idea of covenant making. It is a natural element found in nature; therefore, it fits the idea of being of the earth. It was used to flavor foods; therefore, it was a marketable product. When given as a salary it could then be exchanged at the market rate. It likely was used for different messages at different times. However, it is very natural for the Savior to teach his followers that they are of great worth and purpose. So his use of the metaphor was likely for that purpose at the time.

"a reed shaken with the wind"

When John the Baptist was imprisoned and sent messengers to seek out Jesus and then report back to him, both Luke and Matthew record the account and include in it an idiom. Without knowing the background of the idiom, we are left wondering what Jesus meant:

> 22 Then Jesus answering said unto them, Go your way, and tell John what things ye have seen and heard; how that the blind see, the lame walk, the lepers are cleansed, the deaf hear, the dead are raised, to the poor the gospel is preached.
>
> 23 And blessed is he, whosoever shall not be offended in me.
>
> 24 And when the messengers of John were departed, he began to speak unto the people concerning John, What went ye out into the wilderness for to see? **A reed shaken with the wind**?
>
> 25 But what went ye out for to see? A man clothed in soft raiment? Behold, they which are gorgeously apparelled, and live delicately, are in kings' courts.
>
> 26 But what went ye out for to see? A prophet? Yea, I say unto you, and much more than a prophet.
>
> 27 This is he, of whom it is written, Behold, I send my messenger before thy face, which shall prepare thy way before thee. (Luke 7:22–27; emphasis added. See also Matthew 11:1-15)

If you are aware of a well-known parable told in the time of Jesus about the reed and the oak tree, you could understand why Jesus asked the question "What went ye out to see? **A reed shaken with the wind**?" The parable is of two trees planted near a stream—one an oak tree and the other a reed. The oak tree naturally sent its roots deep, which would make it resilient to the winds. It would withstand most winds while the reed tree would be blown over by the wind even down into the water.

Jesus spoke to the people who had believed John, who was now imprisoned. They questioned why John was not protected from powerful enemies if his mission was so significant. It was to these whom Jesus directed the question, "What went ye out into the wilderness for to see?" The people were expected to conclude that John had been like the oak tree and stood up against all sinners, chief among them Herod, their king. John had not been like the reed and wavered in the wind.

That is why John is paid the most deserving tribute of being much more than a prophet. What a soul-searching question—am I more like the oak or the reed?

"bind up the money in thine hand"

The Lord repeated many points of the laws which were given to the people newly freed from Egypt. He told them that they were a people not like other people and that their daily lives, as well as their rituals, were to be different. He used several idioms within his instructions. One of these was that if they rightly decided to relocate their residence; they should sell and "Then shalt thou turn it into money, and **bind up the money in thine hand,** and shalt go unto the place which the Lord thy God shall choose" (Deuteronomy 14:25; emphasis added).

This counsel is good financial advice for any time. What the Lord is teaching is that they should not spend the revenue on whims, but guard it and spend it carefully. They should "hold on to their money" or "bind up the money in thine hand," and not use it until they were purchasing in another chosen location or estate. Today, a parent may advise a child to do the same thing by saying, "Don't you just blow this money you've acquired. You've got to pinch every penny till you find your new place. You've got to squeeze every nickel and stretch every dollar until you get a chance to bury it in a new place."

"thou shalt have a place also without"

Another practical instruction was given to the people idiomatically. It was to have a place without the camp. The Lord was giving schooling to a people who were used to living in the same locations for decades but were now traveling in the wilderness of Sinai and moving periodically. So he told them, "Thou shalt have a place also without the camp, whither thou shalt go forth abroad" (Deuteronomy 23:12).

The reader of this instruction may not at first identify the idiom or the practical meaning of the same. However, it can be clearly identified that they should have a toilet outside their camp. You should also be able to infer what it means to "go forth abroad." Today we understand the health reasons for such a rule. It was not just an issue of privacy, but of survival and control of disease.

"will send hornets"

Using the characteristics of animals and small creatures is a good method to communicate mannerisms. The Lord said, "And I will send hornets before thee, which shall drive out the Hivite, the Canaanite, and the Hittite, from before thee" (Exodus 23:28). Because today we send "Navy seals," "screaming eagles," and "devil dogs" into combat, we should easily understand that the Lord was directing Moses to send spies or commandoes into the cities before they invaded with their armies. Conquering the city of Jericho with the help of Rahab, who was first contacted by desert raiders sent in by Joshua, was very natural. That is the manner in which hornets attack hives of bees. They send in raiders who are able to kill numerous members of the smaller species and lay claim to their store of food.

"if a fox go up, he shall even break"

Sometimes with sayings or idioms, it is clear that someone must have once said such a thing and over time it became the way to express a message. A fox is not the smallest nor lightest creature, but this metaphor is written, "Now Tobiah the Ammonite was by him, and he said, Even that which they build, if a fox go up, he shall even break down their stone wall" (Nehemiah 4:3).

This was an expression regarding the weakness of the walls of a city. It was a hyperbole saying that a fox would be able to break down their walls. Today we might say, "My mother could whip the whole bunch of them" or "their defense was thin as paper."

"like grasshoppers"

The report of the spies that went to survey the Land of Canaan, brought back a report of fear. They didn't believe that the Lord could help them overcome the peoples embedded and established in the land which the Lord had promised to them. This they believed even though the Lord had freed them from the Egyptian chariots and the waters of the sea. There were twelve spies, and only two of the twelve, Joshua and Caleb, were not in favor of this report that was delivered to Moses. The group reported, "And there we saw the giants, the sons of Anak, which come of the giants: and we were in our own sight as grasshoppers, and so we were in their sight" (Numbers 13:33).

The spies were fearful and considered themselves to be as small as grasshoppers. Today we might express similar feelings when we say, "I can't go up against him. He'll squash me like a bug."

Grasshoppers were also used idiomatically for their vast numbers. "And the Midianites and the Amalekites and all the children of the east lay along in the valley **like grasshoppers** for multitude; and their camels were without number, as the sand by the sea side for multitude" (Judges 7:12; emphasis added).

But grasshoppers were used most often in idioms because of their voracious attacks that devoured even the remains of fields after the harvest. Amos wrote, "Thus hath the Lord God shewed unto me; and, behold, he formed **grasshoppers** in the beginning of the shooting up of the latter growth; and, lo, it was the latter growth after the king's mowings" (Amos 7:1; emphasis added). Amos lived and served in a time of great apostasy. He wondered how Israel could be fruitful when the people of his day were like a field that had already been harvested. They bore little fruit of righteousness. They were even more barren than a harvested field. They were as desolate as a harvested field that had been afterward devoured by hoards of grasshoppers. These were excellent metaphors because they were so common to the people of ancient times.

"they are bread for us"

Joshua, one of the two faithful spies, spoke his own feelings and testimony to Moses and the people. He didn't agree with the report that they were "like grasshoppers" to the people inhabiting Canaan. He used an idiom to tell how he saw the situation. He said, "Only rebel not ye against the Lord, neither fear ye the people of the land; for **they are bread for us**: their defense is departed from them, and the Lord is with us: fear them not" (Numbers 14:9; emphasis added).

He was telling them that they could, with the Lord's help, conquer the people. Today, similar phrases are spoken to bolster confidence when challenging an opponent. It might be said, "We'll eat them alive," we'll "eat their lunch," or "it was like taking candy from a kid." That is the meaning of "they are bread for us."

"spread dung upon your faces."

This idiom is a good example of hyperbole as well as euphemism. It is a phrase that is meant to indicate that shame should be felt because of sinful conduct. Today, it is often said, "he had egg all over his face" which would indicate that embarrassment should be felt because of a poor decision or conduct. This is the same message of "spread dung upon your faces," but just not as dramatic or shameful. Malachi, speaking for God, said the following, "Behold, I will corrupt your seed, and **spread dung upon your faces**, even the dung of your solemn feasts; and one shall take you away with it" (Malachi 2:3; emphasis added).

Jeremiah spoke of a similar time of apostasy. He seems to indicate the shame felt by the earth because of the disobedience of God's people, who inherit the earth. He wrote, "And they shall spread them before the sun, and the moon, and all the host of heaven, whom they have loved, and whom they have served, and after whom they have walked, and whom they have sought, and whom they have worshiped: they shall not be gathered, nor be buried; they shall be for **dung upon the face of the earth**" (Jeremiah 8:2; emphasis added).

"my mouth is enlarged"

A good way today to describe someone who talks a lot, or tells more than should be told, is to say, "You have a big mouth." This is the same message attributed to Hannah when, in her old age, she is informed that she will have a child with promise. Samuel recorded, "And Hannah prayed, and said, My heart rejoiceth in the Lord, mine horn is exalted in the Lord: **my mouth is enlarged** over mine enemies; because I rejoice in thy salvation" (1 Samuel 2:1; emphasis added). In essence she is using a metaphor. She is saying, "Now I can say plenty and defend my barrenness as a mother to my critics who have made me feel it was my fault that I have been childless. Now my mouth is enlarged. I will tell it to everyone and tell the whole story of how I was visited and told I would bear a special child in my old age."

"they that sow in tears shall reap in joy"

Within the often sung hymn of the Church, "We Are Sowing," there words are sung but not often understood. They appear in verses two and four. They are, "Sown in tears and love and prayer" in verse two, and "From the seed we sowed in tears," as the ending of the fourth verse.

2nd verse:
Seeds that fall amid the stillness
Of the lonely mountain glen;
Seeds cast out in crowded places,
Trodden under foot of men;
Seeds by idle hearts forgotten,
Flung at random on the air;
Seeds by faithful souls remembered,
Sown in tears and love and prayer;

4th verse:
Thou who knowest all our weakness,
Leave us not to sow alone!
Bid thine angels guard the furrows
Where the precious grain is sown,
Till the fields are crown'd with glory,
Filled with mellow, ripened ears,
Filled with fruit of life eternal
From the seed we sowed in tears. [2]

Question: "What does sowing seeds have to do with tears?" Answer: Listed below the hymn are two scriptural references. The first mentions nothing about tears. However, the second one does. It reads:

> 1 When the Lord turned again the captivity of Zion, we were like them that dream.
> 2 Then was our mouth filled with laughter, and our tongue with singing: then said they among the heathen, The Lord hath done great things for them.
> 3 The Lord hath done great things for us; whereof we are glad.
> 4 Turn again our captivity, O Lord, as the streams in the south.
> 5 They that sow in tears shall reap in joy.
> 6 He that goeth forth and weepeth, bearing precious seed, shall doubtless come again with rejoicing, bringing his sheaves [with him] (Psalms 126:1–6; emphasis added).

The majority of the Psalms were written or collected by David and then by his son, Solomon. This was before the captivity of Judah, but they had memories of bondage in Egypt as well as under such groups as the Philistines, while in Palestine. But these verses in the Psalms are allegorical, figuratively comparing things we do in life to things that are real. So the words in verse 5 are an idiom. They tell a message just like "Don't count your chickens before they hatch."

To catch the message of "they that sow in tears shall reap in joy," will be difficult for most in our culture, even those who plant crops. This is because we are not like a family in the days of ancient Israel. They had to save some of the present year's harvest in order to have "seed" to plant in the next season. Surpluses were seldom and famine was "always at their door." A father who denied his children the bread that could be made from the seed held for planting, would "sow in tears" while his starving children begged for food. But if he did not withhold the seed from them, they would have no harvest in the future and surely starve to death. From that principle comes the idiom, "they that sow in tears shall reap with joy."

Picture the sacrifices that have been made by those in our past. When Heber C. Kimball and Brigham Young determined that they must answer the call by the Lord to the Twelve Apostles of the Restoration, they left their families who were destitute and sick with the fever and chills. They were so weak themselves that they could hardly walk, so a wagon ride was offered them. They said to themselves that they couldn't leave their destitute, sick families like that, so they weakly stood in the halted wagon and gave their wives a "hurrah for Israel" cheer as they began to make their way to England.[3] There they, as well as others of the Twelve Apostles, planted seeds of the gospel that yielded one of the richest crops ever harvested. The hundreds and then thousands of souls who harkened to their message were the result. These converts brought new life and strength to the Church as it was struggling for existence. The tough sacrifices of parents, teachers, and leaders can all fit in the idiom. Very little of good has come to any of us that has not resulted from the seed "sown in tears," love and prayer.

"a fruitful bough by a well"

Jacob said of his own son Joseph, "Joseph is . . . **a fruitful bough by a well**; whose branches run over the wall" (Genesis 49:22; emphasis added). If you have a plant that lives by a well, there should be little doubt that it will always have life. That is the metaphor spoken to Joseph, that he is by a well, and that his life and posterity would be nourished. It would be nourished because the branches of his offspring or vine would reach out beyond others—they would go over the wall. Today we use similar phrases to indicate certain conditions. We might say that "everything he touches turns to gold," "he's got the Midas touch," or "he must have a gold mine." All of these idioms would indicate wealth and prosperity.

Since Joseph's blessings were to be fulfilled in his two sons, Ephraim and Manasseh (see Genesis 48:15–20), this blessing should be expected to be fulfilled through their descendants. Today, the majority of the members of the tribe of Ephraim, as well as those of Manasseh, enjoy prosperity beyond the dreams of most of the earth's populations. They travel and reside in continents and nations that transcend walls and barriers unlike any other tribe.

"two women shall be in the field"
"two women shall be grinding at the mill"

During Jesus' discourse on the subject of the destruction of Jerusalem and the sign of his coming again, (Matthew 24:1–3), he used a phrase that is idiomatic, not literal. We do not understand the statement because our society is so far changed and our ways of life and subsistence are so removed from those of his day. Jesus made a statement which should be related to both of the questions asked of him. He said, "Then shall **two be in the field**; the one shall be taken, and the other left. **Two women shall be grinding at the mill**; the one shall be taken, and the other left" (Matthew 24:40–41; emphasis added). A literal reading of these two phrases will be of as little help as a literal reading of "a bird in the hand is better than two in the bush."

What Jesus spoke was very clear to people who had been conquered by warring nations. Jerusalem certainly fell into that category. The general procedure for a conquering army was to kill the men who could rebel or fight against them. They let the men and women live who were aged and feeble. They were no threat and they could provide some sustenance before dying, but they could not have offspring so as to perpetuate the conquered nation. The young women and young men were taken to become slaves and workers.

The custom of agrarian, pastoral peoples was to give training to the young. Therefore, fathers were paired with sons so they could be trained. Better yet, young sons were paired with grandfathers. This pairing was beneficial because the young man could supply the heavy work or activity and the older, who likely lacked endurance, could be the teacher and advisor. For women, the same was true. The classic example of a job for an older grandmother, who possibly was blind, would be to feed the grain being ground daily under the wheel and the young girl would push the wheel herself or manage the beast that rotated the grinding wheel. No one who could do anything was idle. There were tasks for the lame and halt, blind and deaf. They would always be paired with someone young to be trained as well as tended.

It is to this condition to which the Savior referred. He said that when Jerusalem would be conquered, two (an old man and a young man) would be in the field. One would be taken and the other left. He said that when Jerusalem was conquered, two (an old woman and a young girl) would be grinding. When this happened, naturally, as anticipated, one would be taken and the other left.

Jesus' dualistic message, for both the destruction of Jerusalem and the separation of the righteous from the unrighteous at his coming, would be natural and expected. He was not trying to give a ratio for salvation nor a value for the old or young. But he taught that the righteous would be taken, just like the conquering nations took those they could use, while they left those that would perish. That is the way it will be at his coming. The separation of the faithful from the unfaithful will be as simple as the division made by the triumphant army. This dualistic answer was understood as well as today's saying, "This will separate the men from the boys." Sometimes, this idiom is used for young men who are the same age. But it has a message that is beyond age or years. It has to do with performance.

"he is in the desert" "he is in the secret chambers" "lightning cometh out of the east"

These are three distinct idioms. They each have their own message. The people living then understood them. Jesus used them all in answering the query of his disciples regarding how they would know of his coming.

25 Behold, I have told you before.

26 Wherefore if they shall say unto you, Behold, **he is in the desert**; go not forth: behold, **he is in the secret chambers**; believe it not.

27 For as the **lightning cometh out of the east**, and shineth even

unto the west; so shall also the coming of the Son of man be" (Matthew 24:25–27; emphasis added).

To be "in the desert" meant that you were denying yourself of needs and pleasures. It is not trying to say you are actually in a barren wasteland, even though you might physically be in such a place. This idiom is semi-transparent. It might literally be so, but that is not the message of the expression. Sometimes a similar statement is that you are in the wilderness. Many have been encouraged to deprive themselves of needs and pleasures if they are to find God. Some believe that they can be closer to God if they are celibate. Others fast for long periods of time; some flagellate themselves or deny themselves of any pleasure. They are told this will bring God to them. Jesus said to such, "Go not forth." By responding with that answer, he was saying that undergoing depravation was not the process by which a person would find God. To be without certain pleasures may help you in your quest, but many feel that you cannot find God unless you separate yourself from all pleasure and passion. Today, you may express your hope for someone who is wayward by saying, "Let's send him to live with grandma. Up in her little town, they roll up all the streets at sundown and turn off the electricity right after supper. He'll come around." The saying "I'll find God in the desert" is the same idea.

Jesus also warned against believing those who would say "he is in the secret chambers." This suggests that you will find God in secret meetings and secret places. Such an idea goes against what Paul said to Agrippa and Festus. Paul said that the teachings of Christ and his resurrection were "not done in a corner." Christ did everything in public or "upon the housetops." To the notion of such secret places wherein only a few will find God, Jesus said, "Believe it not."

But if you really want to know of the Lord's coming, compare it to something everyone knows about. It is the coming up of the sun each and every day. There are indicators as to the rising of the sun. First the sun gives off light into the sky long before you ever see the sun. To nearly every spot on the earth, it is predictable that the sun will rise from the east, north of east, or south of east. But if you watch the seasons, and if you know from whence the sun rose yesterday or last year, on a certain date, you can be assured that the sun will rise from that direction again. So what are the indications that the sun is preparing to rise? The words of the beautiful hymn "The Day Dawn Is Breaking" makes a comparison of things happening now caused by the Restoration, to the things that signal the time just before the rising of the sun, which begins the beautiful millennial day. Pick them out of the verses of the hymn—notice the italics.

1st verse:
The day dawn is breaking, the world is awaking,
The clouds of night's darkness are fleeing away.
The worldwide commotion, from ocean to ocean,
Now heralds the time of the beautiful day.

Chorus:
Beautiful day of peace and rest,
Bright be thy dawn from east to west.
Hail to thine earliest welcome ray,
Beautiful, bright, millennial day.

2nd verse:
In many a temple the saints will assemble
And labor as saviors of dear ones away.
Then happy reunion and sweetest communion
We'll have with our friends in the beautiful day.

3rd verse:
Still let us be doing, our lessons reviewing,
Which God has revealed for our walk in his way;
And then wondrous story, the Lord in his glory
Will come in his power in the beautiful day."[4]

The message of the hymn "The Spirit of God," also lists elements heralding the glorious day of the Lord's coming.

1st verse:
The spirit of God like a fire is burning!
The latter-day glory begins to come forth;
The visions and blessings of old are returning,
And angels are coming to visit the earth.

2nd verse:

The Lord *is extending the saints' understanding,*
Restoring their judges and all as at first.
The knowledge and power of God are expanding;
The veil o'er the earth is beginning to burst.

3rd verse:

We'll call in our solemn assemblies in spirit,
To spread forth the kingdom of heaven a broad,
That we through our faith may begin to inherit
The visions and blessings and glories of God.[5]

Members of the Church often comment that the Savior will come in his return from the east. They arrive at this conclusion from verse 27 of Matthew, chapter 24. They also are inclined to conclude the same from traditional practices such as burying our dead facing east and some temples with their main doors facing east. However, careful reading of verse 27 will show that the Savior was making a metaphor or analogy relating to his coming. He was saying that there would be things to notice before the dawn of his coming, not the direction from which he would come. If he meant it literally that he would come from the east, that would make certain things rather difficult, such as living at either of the poles of the earth. We have many traditions and practices which are both literal and metaphorical, such as wearing a wedding ring on the "ring finger" of the left hand, bowing our head during prayer, men removing a cap or hat from their heads during prayer, and blessing food before it is eaten. We do these things to teach us principles, doctrines, and reverence, even though they are not a literal requirement.

"wheresoever the carcase is, there will the eagles be gathered together"

Continuing with Jesus' list of indicators regarding his return, we need to consider the next idiom, "For wheresoever the carcase is, there will the eagles be gathered together" (Matthew 24:28). Joseph Smith made several changes to this verse. He made it to read, *"And now I show unto you a parable.* Behold, **wheresoever the carcass is, there will the eagles be gathered together;** *so likewise shall mine elect be gathered from the four quarters of the earth"* (JST—Matthew 1:27; emphasis added and parts Joseph Smith added are in italics).

This idiom being discussed is another metaphor. Jesus said the idiom was a parable, and therefore should be understood by those reading or hearing the parable. When you see eagles, other birds of prey, or scavengers gathering, you know there is a creature dead or near death nearby. Then he made the metaphor or comparison that his elect would be gathered from the four quarters of the earth. This doctrine of the gathering is one of the most prominent beliefs and practices of the restored Church of Jesus Christ. "We believe in the literal gathering of Israel and in the restoration of the Ten Tribes" (Article of Faith 10).

Anyone who wants to see an evidence of this literal fulfillment needs only to observe Saints meeting in the same manner, believing the same doctrines, having the same correlated lessons, all over the wide expanses of most of the earth. If another example is needed, twice a year general conference of the Church is held in Salt Lake City. However, it is not just the large gathering in Salt Lake City that should be observed, but it should be recognized that the messages from Salt Lake City are being broadcast to chapels and homes in millions of locations around the world where saints have gathered. The broadcasts and publications of the conference proceedings are in a multitude of languages. If you were to attend the conference in Salt Lake City, you would see and hear saints who have come from regions all over the earth. They speak their own languages and have gathered to feast on the same "carcass."

Notes

1. "Come, Come Ye Saints," *Hymns* no. 30.
2. "We Are Sowing," *Hymns* no. 216.
3. See Joseph Smith, *History of The Church of Jesus Christ of Latter-day Saints* (Salt Lake City: Deseret News, 1904), 18.
4. "The Day Dawn Is Breaking," *Hymns* no. 52.
5. "The Spirit of God," *Hymns* no. 2.

IDIOMS REGARDING GENDER

"pisseth against the wall"

This expression seems crude or vulgar. However, it was a clear action done only by males since doing such is functional for males, not females. It was clearly a euphemism, or an idiom, that refers to adult males. It is another way of separating all females from the event. According to the record, the idiom was used by the Lord: "Therefore, behold, I will bring evil upon the house of Jeroboam, and will cut off from Jeroboam him that **pisseth against the wall**, and him that is shut up and left in Israel, and will take away the remnant of the house of Jeroboam, as a man taketh away dung, till it be all gone" (1 Kings 14:10; emphasis added. See also 1 Kings 21:21; 1 Samuel 25:22, 34; 2 Kings 9:8).

All these Old Testament statements point toward having a posterity or an inheritance. However, without males this is an impossibility, but the sense of such statements also deals with a righteous posterity. Note how the Lord speaks about those who are fighting against his work during the latter days and the work of Joseph Smith: "And not many years hence, that they and their posterity shall be swept from under heaven, saith God, that not one of them is left to **stand by the wall**" (D&C 121:15; emphasis added). Here the full idiom is not used. However, the setting for section 121 that contains the decree begins with Joseph's prayer, which he offered while suffering with others of

God's servants, as they were illegally imprisoned by vile men in Liberty, Missouri, in 1839. Being able "to stand" as well as "standing by the wall" are both idioms that carry a message and a connotation of worthiness and inheriting. They are the opposite of "upon thy belly." Those who are to inherit kingdoms of righteousness will "stand before God" and be witnesses and heirs. Notice the message the Lord gives in the record of Luke. "Watch ye therefore, and pray always, that ye may be accounted worthy to escape all these things that shall come to pass, and to stand before the Son of man" (Luke 21:36).

Joseph Smith adds to Luke's record, "And what I say unto one, I say unto all, Watch ye therefore, and pray always, and keep my commandments, that ye may be counted worthy to escape all these things which shall come to pass, and **to stand** before the Son of man when he shall come clothed in the glory of his Father" (JST Luke 21:36; emphasis added).

Consistent with this message of standing before God, and being worthy to testify and inherit are the words in another revelation to Joseph Smith. The Lord said, "He that is slothful shall not be counted **worthy to stand**, and he that learns not his duty and shows himself not approved shall not be counted **worthy to stand**. Even so. Amen" (D&C 107:100; emphasis added).

"spilled it on the ground"

This idiom is a euphemism. "And Onan knew that the seed should not be his; and it came to pass, when he went in unto his brother's wife, that he **spilled it on the ground**, lest that he should give seed to his brother" (Genesis 38:9; emphasis added). This is a form of birth control. It means that a man would withdraw himself and let his semen not go into his sexual cohort.

"unclean"

The word *unclean* seems to indicate a condition of filthiness or sinfulness; however, it is a designation that is more general. It should be considered as "to be avoided" or "separated from others." The reason to be separated from others varies. Sometimes it is for physical safety, other times it is for spiritual safety, and still other times it is to teach a doctrine. These are illustrated as follows:

The touching of a dead creature, human or animal, made the

person who touched it unclean. The cause of death may or may not be known and its contagiousness not yet evident. Therefore, whatever or whomever touched anything dead was considered "unclean." Sin was not the issue, but safety was. This was the case of leprosy, thought of as "living death."

"Unclean spirits" could be harmful to the soul. Those who taught evil or incorrect doctrines should be avoided. Jesus, knowing that his apostles would encounter such in their ministry charged them, "And he called unto him the twelve, and began to send them forth by two and two; and gave them power over unclean spirits" (Mark 6:7).

To teach a principle, such as the distinction between maleness and femaleness, the account reads;

1 And the Lord spake unto Moses, saying,

2 Speak unto the children of Israel, saying, If a woman have conceived seed, and born a **man child**: then she shall be **unclean seven days**; according to the days of the separation for her infirmity shall she be unclean.

3 And in the eighth day the flesh of his foreskin shall be circumcised.

4 And she shall then continue in the blood of her purifying three and thirty days; she shall touch no hallowed thing, nor come into the sanctuary, until the days of her purifying be fulfilled.

5 But if she bear a **maid child**, then she shall be **unclean two weeks**, as in her separation: and she shall continue in the blood of her purifying threescore and six days.

6 And when the days of her purifying are fulfilled, for a son, or for a daughter, she shall bring a lamb of the first year for a burnt offering, and a young pigeon, or a turtledove, for a sin offering, unto the door of the tabernacle of the congregation, unto the priest:

7 Who shall offer it before the Lord, and make an atonement for her; and she shall be cleansed from the issue of her blood. **This is the law for her that hath born a male or a female**.

8 And if she be not able to bring a lamb, then she shall bring two turtles, or two young pigeons; the one for the burnt offering, and the other for a sin offering: and the priest shall make an atonement for her, and she shall be clean (Leviticus 12:1–8; emphasis added).

Setting aside the doctrine of "original sin" and its evil ramifications, there is no sin for the maid child, the man child, nor for the mother when childbirth occurs. However, the mother is to be separated because of the issue of blood that occurs with the process of birth. Blood is the fluid that the body uses to transport all infection. So the mother is to be separate until her menstrual time comes and concludes—and any issue of blood and fluids cease. This period was extended if her birth involved a maid child. Not for safety, but for teaching a principle.

To be "unclean" is more about separation than the need to be cleansed. However, the reason to separate may be because of sin and evil. In his last words as he completed the book named for his father, Moroni said, "And again I would exhort you that ye would come unto Christ, and lay hold upon every good gift, and touch not the evil gift, nor the unclean thing" (Moroni 10:30).

The Lord also stated in the Law, "And that ye may put difference between holy and unholy, and between unclean and clean" (Leviticus 10:10). Holiness and cleanliness were associated with each other but just because one is not clean, it does not mean that he is unholy. But people know what it is like to be dirty. They also know how to cleanse themselves. So sin was easily associated with being unclean; however, it did not guarantee a connection. Today we can be caught "red handed" and our hands are just fine. We can speak with a "forked tongue" and have no deformity. We can be "two faced" and not be sinful, just "double minded." We might even be a "dirty rat" and yet not be sinful, but just someone to be avoided. The term "unclean" implies more than filthiness. But it was an idiom that was often spoken and was just one word, a word that could result in much activity. Just like "Fire" being yelled in the theater or speaking the word *bomb* in an airport.

"a man is born into the world"

To those living in Western culture, some of the customs of Eastern cultures are unfathomable. The requirements for women to always cover their faces and not be able to vote, speak, or own property are hard to believe. However, that does not change the reality of their existence. We know of the efforts of the Egyptians to suppress the birthrate of Israelite male children during their bondage. The Egyptians ordered the midwives to take away the life of each male child at birth. Additionally we know the edict of King Herod wherein he ordered the killing of all the male children in Bethlehem. These atrocities seem beyond belief. We wish that our present-day values could have been applicable at that time. Nevertheless, we should be aware of other such prevailing customs of Bible times.

For example, during the time of Jesus, and for centuries previous, the birth of girls was not welcomed. A woman was not satisfied until she had given birth to a male child to carry on the name and posterity of her husband. If during childbirth the life of the mother is endangered, and if the child born to her was a male child, she was told the news, hoping it would revive her and give her reason to live. If the child was a female, the gender was often not told to the woman for fear that the unhappiness would take away her desire to live.

Catch the message of Jesus to his disciples and his use of this idiomatic expression to teach them how they should feel:

> 16 A little while, and ye shall not see me: and again, a little while, and ye shall see me, because I go to the Father.
>
> 17 Then said some of his disciples among themselves, What is this that he saith unto us, A little while, and ye shall not see me: and again, a little while, and ye shall see me: and, Because I go to the Father?
>
> 18 They said therefore, What is this that he saith, A little while? we cannot tell what he saith.
>
> 19 Now Jesus knew that they were desirous to ask him, and said unto them, Do ye enquire among yourselves of that I said, A little while, and ye shall not see me: and again, a little while, and ye shall see me?
>
> 20 Verily, verily, I say unto you, That ye shall weep and lament, but the world shall rejoice: and ye shall be sorrowful, but your sorrow shall be turned into joy.
>
> 21 A woman when she is in travail hath sorrow, because her hour is come: but as soon as she is delivered of the child, she remembereth no more the anguish, for joy that **a man is born into the world**.
>
> 22 And ye now therefore have sorrow: but I will see you again, and your heart shall rejoice, and your joy no man taketh from you (John 16:16–22; emphasis added).

Jesus compared their fears to a mother giving birth. She is worried about the possibility of her child being not a male, just like his disciples were worried about Jesus not being the messiah. Because of this idiom, used in his day, his disciples would know that Jesus was comparing this time in his mission to the time of a mother preparing to give birth, and not knowing if her child would be male or female. He assured them. He said that their "sorrow shall be turned into joy." He compared their gaining assurance that he truly was the Messiah, to a mother in childbirth being told that "a man is born into the world." His disciples would know of his true messiahship when he came back to life through his power of resurrection.

It seems that this same process applies to what the Lord told Brigham Young. The Lord made reference regarding the wicked who had rejected Joseph Smith and the restoration. The Lord declared: "And now cometh the day of their calamity, even the days of sorrow, like a **woman that is taken in travail**; and their **sorrow shall be great** unless they speedily repent, yea, very speedily" (D&C 136:35; emphasis added).

The Lord, through Brigham Young, was indicating that the anguish of the unbelievers of the restored truths given to Joseph Smith would be as sorrowful as a woman who does not give birth to a man child, thus not having a posterity for herself nor her husband. Even in the time of Brigham Young, the Lord still used an idiom from long ago. Understanding what the Lord said requires understanding the distant past and customs experienced by peoples far removed from our time.

IDIOMS
REGARDING BELIEF
AND DOCTRINE

"deny himself" "take up his cross"

The Savior taught that his followers should deny themselves. "Then said Jesus unto his disciples, If any man will come after me, let him deny himself, and take up his cross, and follow me" (Matthew 16:24). Both Mark and Luke wrote that the Savior also said that everyone who came after him should take up his cross.

- "And when he had called the people unto him with his disciples also, he said unto them, Whosoever will come after me, let him **deny himself**, and **take up his cross**, and follow me" (Mark 8:34; emphasis added).
- "And he said to them all, If any man will come after me, let him **deny himself**, and **take up his cross** daily, and follow me" (Luke 9:23; emphasis added).

These two idioms, "deny himself" and "take up his cross" are buried in the liturgy of Christianity. They have taken the forms of celibacy, lent, and wearing of the cross, among others. Careful consideration of the changes made by the Prophet Joseph Smith, noted in the footnotes to Matthew 16:24, will lead to a more enlightened understanding regarding the true doctrines in these two idioms. Joseph noted that "the meaning of the phrase 'to take up the cross of Jesus is to deny ungodliness" (see JST Matthew 16:24). He rendered the following verses,

25 Then said Jesus unto his disciples, If any man will come after me, let him deny himself, and take up his cross, and follow me.

26 And now for a man to take up his cross, is to deny himself all ungodliness, and every worldly lust, and keep my commandments. (JST Matthew 16:25–26)

This understanding is consistent with what Moroni taught. He entreated: "Yea, come unto Christ, and be perfected in him, and deny yourselves of all ungodliness; and if ye shall deny yourselves of all ungodliness, and love God with all your might, mind and strength, then is his grace sufficient for you, that by his grace ye may be perfect in Christ; and if by the grace of God ye are perfect in Christ, ye can in nowise deny the power of God" (Moroni 10:32; see also JST Matthew 5:31 and JST Mark 8:40). All of these show a dissimilar meaning for these two idioms than is generally observed in Christian thinking.

By correctly understanding this idiom to deny ourselves of all unrighteousness, it is helpful when we read the one-time use of a similar idiom in all of scripture. It appears in the book of Alma wherein Alma counsels his wayward son Corianton, and said, "Now my son, I would that ye should repent and forsake your sins, and go no more after the lusts of your eyes, but **cross yourself** in all these things; for except ye do this ye can in nowise inherit the kingdom of God. Oh, remember, and take it upon you, and **cross yourself** in these things" (Alma 39:9; emphasis added). This idiom, though not found in the Bible, has a much different meaning in the liturgy of other prominent Christian churches. However, the message of all these idioms is consistent and clear as to their meaning if we apply the additional explanations offered in the JST.

"thorn in the flesh"

Regarding the denying oneself of certain pleasures, the Apostle Paul's statement about having a "thorn in the flesh" enters into the question. Some wonder what evil, physical, or moral weakness afflicted the apostle. He wrote:

7 And lest I should be exalted above measure through the abundance of the revelations, there was given to me a **thorn in the flesh**, the messenger of Satan to buffet me, lest I should be exalted above measure.

8 For this thing I besought the Lord thrice, that it might depart from me.

9 And he said unto me, My grace is sufficient for thee: for my strength is made perfect in weakness. Most gladly therefore will I rather glory in my infirmities, that the power of Christ may rest upon me.

10 Therefore I take pleasure in infirmities, in reproaches, in necessities, in persecutions, in distresses for Christ's sake: for when I am weak, then am I strong. (2 Corinthians 12:7–10; emphasis added).

Many have interpreted that Paul had something in his life or past wherein he had not denied himself in some manner and therefore was subjected to incessant temptation. Some have chosen to believe that Paul had chronic maladies such as eye problems, while others believe his problem may have been malaria, migraine headaches, epilepsy, or a disability of speech. However, properly understanding what the Savior taught regarding "to deny himself" as well as knowing the accepted present-day expectations of an apostle, we should not look for personal sins as this "thorn in the flesh" spoken of by Paul.

Considering this phrase as an idiom should guide us to something which bothered Paul and to which he hade metaphoric reference—not an actual malady. He did write that three times he had besought the Lord that it would depart from him. If we consider his calling as the thing from which he wished relief, he would not be alone in such a wish. Others have asked God to relieve them of the calling to which they have been appointed. Moses wished he could be relieved of leading a rebellious disobedient people in the wilderness. Joseph Smith begged God to not have to instigate plural marriage. Wilford Woodruff wished that he did not have to be the one to issue the manifesto ending plural marriages that even included his own. They all asked that their lives be taken rather than do as commanded. Possibly Paul was not asking for a malady to be removed from him, but a situation and a call that he found anguishing and burdensome.

By reading his epistles, we can identify Paul's problematic topic of discussion with both Jews and non-Jews. The topic was the doctrine regarding circumcision. Paul had found out that his circumcision was of no value to him and other Jews. Therefore this was always a "thorn" that Paul wished he did not have. It put him squarely where the unbelieving Jews would have him—as one of them. They practiced circumcision as part of the Law of Moses. When Paul attempted to teach them that the Law of Moses had been fulfilled, the fact that he was circumcised made his message fall on deaf ears. They believed that obeying the Law of Moses was the ultimate performance to God, rather than seeing it as a law that would go away. So Paul's circumcision, as part of his upbringing under the Law of Moses, was a "thorn in the flesh" to him. When he taught Jews, he wished he was not circumcised! When he was teaching Gentiles, his circumcision made him a Jew in their minds. He had a difficult time causing them to believe that circumcision did not matter any more since he had followed the Law of Moses most of his life. He wished that he could teach Christ's mission and message without this burden. Sometimes leaders have problem members that trouble them. They are a "burr under their saddle," or a "fly in the ointment."

It is more sound to look at this phrase as figurative, the same as his "run the race" analogies. I find it beyond wonder as to why scholars have not chosen to select the most burdensome condition with which Paul had to deal as a possibility for his "thorn in the flesh." To conclude that Paul made reference to his situation but did not identify it is not as plausible as believing that the problem and the answer both lie within what he wrote to people not in his presence. They would have to know of his trouble through previous visits or by the epistles themselves. The Jewish/gentile question was ever before him. He could complain about it for he had not chosen circumcision. His parents had seen to that. He always had to deal with it. Circumcision, or the implications of it, appears in almost every one of Paul's letters and discussions. It was truly a thorn in his side or flesh.

"Son of Man"

Most Bible commentators or interpreters consider this phrase as an idiom. However, revelations additional to the Bible show that it is, first, a proper name. It has been misinterpreted as simply an indicator that Jesus or mortals are sons of man. However, revealed truths in addition to the Bible will show otherwise. Bruce R. McConkie published the following summary:

> The whole body of revealed writ attests to the eternal verity that the Supreme God is a Holy Man. "In the language of Adam," the Mosaic account recites, "Man of Holiness is his name, and the name of his Only Begotten is the Son of Man, even Jesus Christ." (Moses 6:57.) Thus, when Jesus asked the ancient disciples, "Whom do men say that I the Son of man am?" (Matthew 16:13), it was as though he

asked: "Who do men say that I am? I testify that I am the Son of Man of Holiness, which is to say, the Son of that Holy Man who is God, but who do men say that I am?" In this same vein, one of the early revelations given in this dispensation asks: "What is the name of God in the pure language?" The answer: "Ahman." Question: "What is the name of the Son of God?" Answer: "Son Ahman." (Orson Pratt, cited in Mormon Doctrine 2nd ed., p. 29) And to Enoch the Lord identified himself by saying: "Behold, I am God; Man of Holiness is my name; Man of Counsel is my name; and Endless and Eternal is my name, also." (Moses 7:35)[1]

In conclusion, "Son of Man" is an idiom, but it is also a proper name for Jesus Christ. Many other names for Jesus Christ are idioms; such as: "Lamb of God," "The Anointed One," "Bread of Life," "Living Water," and "The Word."

"sons of God" "daughters of men"

This phrase has also not been properly handled by translators nor scholars. Furthermore, modern revelations give us the key and understanding of its implications. It appears early in the biblical account. During the apostate years preceding the flood, it is used to indicate the degree to which disobedience has occurred. We read, "That the **sons of God** saw the **daughters of men** that they were fair; and they took them wives of all which they chose" (Genesis 6:2; emphasis added).

In one sense, all sons are sons of God, and all daughters are daughters of men. However, there are distinctions that need to be noted. To be a son of God, one must do more than just exist. John began his gospel by identifying who Jesus was. He indicated that Jesus lived before this life and even was the Creator of worlds. Jesus came as the Word, and we must gain faith in him. He said, "But as many as received him, to them gave he power to become the sons of God, even to them that believe on his name" (John 1:12).

As assurance of the process of becoming a son of God, Jesus spoke to the Nephites after his crucifixion and said, "And as many as have received me, to them have I given to become the **sons of God**; and even so will I to as many as shall believe on my name, for behold, by me redemption cometh, and in me is the law of Moses fulfilled" (3 Nephi 9:17; emphasis added).

The same blessing is promised to daughters who believe. To Emma

Smith the word of the Lord came, "Hearken unto the voice of the Lord your God, while I speak unto you, Emma Smith, my daughter; for verily I say unto you, all those who receive my gospel **are sons and daughters** in my kingdom" (D&C 25:1; emphasis added).

So the message of Genesis 6:2 was this: that men who believed in God were looking upon daughters who did not believe in God. This is why the women were called "daughters of men." The problem came when the "sons of God" began taking the "daughters of men" in marriage, as recorded in Moses: "And when these men began to multiply on the face of the earth, and daughters were born unto them, the sons of men saw that those daughters were fair, and they took them wives, even as they chose. And the Lord said unto Noah: The daughters of thy sons have sold themselves; for behold mine anger is kindled against the sons of men, for they will not hearken to my voice" (Moses 8:14–15).

What the Lord said to benefit Hyrum Smith in 1829 strongly teaches the same message. "But verily, verily, I say unto you, that as many as receive me, to them will I give power to become the sons of God, even to them that believe on my name. Amen" (D&C 11:30). Men who follow God will become holders of the priesthood. Therefore the idiom "sons of God" can be appropriately applied to holders of the priesthood and may have been the additional intent in the idiom noted in Genesis (see also Moroni 7:26, 48; D&C 34:3; 35:2; Moses 7:1).

"cleave unto his wife"

The meaning of the word *cleave* is to separate. If there is cleavage then there is separation. To read the command to Adam and Eve it is natural for many to define the word as "cling" or "hold" rather than separate. God said, "Therefore shall a man leave his father and his mother, and shall cleave unto his wife: and they shall be one flesh" (Genesis 2:24). In the revelation known as "The Law," the Lord gave the same instruction, "Thou shalt love thy wife with all thy heart, and shalt cleave unto her and none else" (D&C 42:22).

Since "cleave unto her" is an idiom, it has messages that do not necessarily match the words and the way they are used. However, if we know the definition of the word is to be separate, then we should know what God is commanding. He is instructing men to make their wife separate from all others and treat her separate. If we cleave the wood, we split it. If the butcher chops the meat, he uses a meat cleaver. If a man cleaves unto his wife, he gives no attention to any other woman in the manner he covenanted to have with his wife.

"one flesh"

If the meaning of cleave is unclear, perhaps the meaning and nature of being one needs clarification. The best definition of the number one is exclusion.[2] It has such a tendency to be considered for its message of unity that the question, "Which comes first, unity or exclusion?" is not answered. You cannot have unity unless you exclude. You might have exclusion and still not have unity. God is saying that we must be exclusive with our wives. If we are exclusive in our feelings, presence, thoughts, and desires, then we are one. The idiom goes far beyond being exclusive sexually. Sin occurs prior to being sexually unfaithful. If we are not "one flesh," we are not exclusive in one or more ways that we have been commanded to be. Jesus taught to "have an eye single" and our whole body would be filled with light (See Matthew 6:22). That is another idiom. It has meaning which goes beyond the meaning of the words themselves. Such is the case of "one flesh."

"whosoever shall marry her that is divorced" Matthew 5:32

This is one of the least understood statements in scripture. It has been doctrinally scrutinized by authorities in every church because people want to know how they should feel about the doctrines regarding divorce and marriage. The Catholic Church has stood by its uncompromising interpretation to the degree that church members live apart from their marriage partners without divorce and cohabit with other partners just so they do not violate the law of the church and the interpretation of the verses which read:

> 31 It hath been said, Whosoever shall put away his wife, let him give her a writing of divorcement:
> 32 But I say unto you, That whosoever shall put away his wife, saving for the cause of fornication, causeth her to commit adultery: and **whosoever shall marry her that is divorced committeth adultery**."
> (Matthew 5:31–32; emphasis added)

Members of most protestant churches are not under such penalties as those evoked by the Catholic Church, but they are left to interpret the doctrine for themselves or follow the counsel and interpretation of their spiritual priest. However, this does not answer the question of what the Savior meant in his teaching.

For many perplexing statements like this one within the sermon on the mount, members of the restored Church of Jesus Christ will compare the same sermon given in the Book of Mormon by the resurrected Lord hoping to find clarification as they have done for many other questions. However, the verses found in 3 Nephi 12:31–32 read precisely the same as Jesus' words in Matthew. Some ask, "Why is there no difference when obviously the statement does not seem to reflect accepted Church doctrine and practice?"

George M. Lamsa, a native Assyrian, was reared speaking Aramaic and experiencing many unchanged customs and sayings in his culture that have continued since Bible times. Converted to Christianity in the early part of the twentieth century, he found that his native understanding of language and customs were helpful in understanding the translations of the Bible that had been made into English. Regarding divorce he clarified the problem by saying that in Aramaic, which both Western and Eastern scholars agree, was the native language of Jesus, there are three words regarding divorce. In English, there is only one word for the process. The three Aramaic words are: *nishbook*, which means to leave and separate; *nishry*, which means to actually divorce; and *shiriana*, which means a writing of divorcement.[3] So the words in Matthew, written in the English text, lack the clarity of the Eastern Aramaic text on the same subject. Let us plug into the English text of Matthew these Aramaic words and their meanings.

> 31 It hath been said, Whosoever shall put away his wife, let him give her a **writing of divorcement: [*shiriana*]**
>
> 32 But I say unto you, That whosoever **shall put away [*nishbook*— meaning simply to separate]** his wife, saving for the cause of fornication, causeth her to commit adultery: and whosoever shall marry her **that is divorced [*nishbook*—separated, not divorced]** committeth adultery.

The problem is solved! Using English, we think of nishry (divorce) each time the process of separating, legally divorcing, and documenting the divorce occurs. But it matches all other teachings of Jesus and the Church if the English text reads that whosoever shall marry her that is separated (nishbook) commits adultery. There is no reason to change the Matthew or the 3 Nephi accounts—they are correct. We just needed enough information regarding the language in which the

Savior taught to have the doctrines he taught not seemingly conflict with other principles and practices taught and practiced in the present-day Church.

"beware of dogs"

If someone says "she has the eye of an eagle" they do not intend for us to consider that she has had an eye transplant. But if the characteristics of an eagle and its eye are known, then we have the key to knowing that she can see even the smallest thing that takes place. So to understand an idiom one must consider the common characteristics of the main element in the idiom. Since the word *beware* is included before the word *dog*, "man's best friend" should not come to mind as the objective of the idiom. However, knowing that dogs are vicious would be the more likely message in the saying. One of the most vicious things that is evil is to gossip. Paul told the saints to: "**Beware of dogs**, beware of evil workers, beware of the concision" (Philippians 3:2; emphasis added). He was warning them to beware of gossipers for they are viscous. We are warned often to "beware of wolves in sheep's clothing." We are told to not go on "witch hunts." Criminals are told to fear "the long arm of the law." So it does not seem unusual for Paul to warn Saints of "dogs." They understood that he spoke of gossiping.

"shake off the dust of your feet"

During much of biblical times, when you welcomed someone into your dwelling place, it was customary to provide water for your guest to wash his feet. Seating, such as today with chairs and tables, was uncommon. To be seated on chairs your feet are below you and often out of sight. Likewise tables would conceal your feet. But when seated on the ground, your feet would often be extended forward toward your host or other guests. It was proper that your feet be clean and free from the filth of the streets or paths of your journey so all could feel pleasant. If you were not welcomed, then you were not provided such formality of washing and had to shake off the dust of your feet. It became an idiom like ours today, "I had to carry my own bags." This could be done literally but was also thought of figuratively.

Today we use idioms indicating rejection or insult. Some are, "They walked all over us," "They spit on all our ideas," or "What they said was a slap in the face." Such sayings, though possibly real, likely did not physically happen. But the idioms tell a message. The same message occurs with the "providing water" or the opposite idea, to "shake off the dust of your feet with no water." Metaphorically it carried the message of rejection. Therefore you should have nothing to do with those who spurned your visit and have nothing to do with their philosophies that caused them to not receive you. Jesus taught, "And whosoever shall not receive you, nor hear your words, when ye depart out of that house or city, **shake off the dust of your feet**" (Matthew 10:14; emphasis added).

The same idiom is still used in recent times and therefore not understood because customs have changed. The Lord instructed in 1832: "And in whatsoever house ye enter, and they receive you not, ye shall depart speedily from that house, and shake off the dust of your feet as a testimony against them" (D&C 75:20). Previously, the Lord had instructed, "And shake off the dust of thy feet against those who receive thee not, not in their presence, lest thou provoke them, but in secret; and wash thy feet, as a testimony against them in the day of judgment" (D&C 60:15).

In the day of judgment, the rejection of the testimony of servants of God will be the issue. It will not be whether or not the servants' feet were literally washed or shaken. Today, idioms are still used to indicate welcoming as well as rejection. Some are given "the key to the city" or the "red carpet treatment." Others have the "door slammed in their face" or "get a poke in the eye." Every missionary should understand the idiomatic instructions by the Lord regarding "to shake off the dust of your feet." It need not be actually performed any more than "putting your shoulder to the wheel." But an attitude or way to feel regarding the situation is the objective. Often when something should be removed from our thinking, we are told to "just drop it." That action is no more literal than if they "received you with open arms," or "turned their back" to you. The metaphors for receiving and rejecting are the same for giving water with which to wash the feet, and having to shake the dust off your feet as a witness of your reception as servants of God.

"shall take up serpents" "drink any deadly thing" "leaven of the "Pharisees"

Snakes are reptiles that often poison and bring about death. References are recurrently made of people because they mimic or imitate animals or other creatures. One might be called a jackass, a monkey, a snake, a mule, a hyena, a wolf, or any one of dozens of other creatures because of their familiar features and actions. What better way to tell you what would happen to you if you were around deadly things? Today we might say that one has been bitten by the "gambling bug." It is so descriptive to hear that someone has been bitten by or poisoned by pornography.

The Savior instructed his disciples to go out and teach the people. They would encounter those who taught doctrines that would lead to spiritual death. He warned and assured them that, "They **shall take up serpents**; and if they **drink any deadly thing**, it shall not hurt them: they shall lay hands on the sick, and they shall recover" (Mark 16:18; emphasis added). The literal reading of these verses has led to some Christian groups handling snakes as part of their religious practice and doctrine. They not only handle venomous snakes, but if they are bitten, they refuse medical attention. They profess that if they have enough faith and personal righteousness, they will not die from the poisonous venom. Deaths and lawsuits have resulted, all because of these scriptural misunderstandings.

The same instructions were given to disciples who lived in the time of Mormon. He reported, "And these signs shall follow them that believe—in my name shall they cast out devils; they shall speak with new tongues; they shall take up serpents; and if they drink any deadly thing it shall not hurt them; they shall lay hands on the sick and they shall recover" (Mormon 9:24).

It should be no surprise for God to warn us about the poisons of enemies. "Then Jesus said unto them, Take heed and beware of the leaven of the Pharisees and of the Sadducees" (Matthew 16:6). The "leaven of the Pharisees" is another idiom not to be taken literally. It displays the effect leaven has on bread and other foods. Evidently his disciples did not fully understand the connection, so Jesus asked, "How is it that ye do not understand that I spake it not to you concerning bread, that ye should beware of the leaven of the Pharisees and of the Sadducees? Then understood they how that he bade them not beware of the leaven of bread, but of the doctrine of the Pharisees and of the Sadducees" (Matthew 16:11–12).

Herod was the Jewish ruler placed in power by the Romans who did not want to lose his political power. Herod would not believe Jesus.

So Mark's account tells what the Savior said to his disciples, "And he charged them, saying, Take heed, beware of the leaven of the Pharisees, and of the leaven of Herod" (Mark 8:15).

Instructions to ministers of the gospel in the latter-days from the same Jesus Christ have not changed. He instructed, "Require not miracles, except I shall command you, except casting out devils, healing the sick, and against poisonous serpents, and against deadly poisons" (D&C 24:13).

Concerning those individuals who go about the Lord's work Jesus taught, "And these signs shall follow him—he shall heal the sick, he shall cast out devils, and shall be delivered from those who would administer unto him deadly poison" (D&C 124:98).

The deadly poisons in all these references are the teachings or doctrines of false teachers who should be considered as enemies. Their venom will kill the soul. The only anti-venom is true doctrine, which Jesus has taught to all of his faithful servants everywhere. Jesus also taught: "Behold, I give unto you power to **tread on serpents and scorpions,** and over all the power of the enemy: and nothing shall by any means hurt you" (Luke 10:19; emphasis added). Treading on poisonous creatures is metaphoric for overcoming them with true doctrine. Many times missionaries and other servants do just that—put down doctrines that would kill the soul. They "walk all over" the adversary and thus overcome the evil that is before them.

"breathed on them"

Certain actions described in the scriptural record do not adhere to accepted Church procedure but create a mystical scenario. If taken literally, the following instance raises questions as to what the Savior did, "And when he had said this, he breathed on them, and saith unto them, Receive ye the Holy Ghost" (John 20:22). Once again, if there is an idiom, it needs to be identified. The idiom is he "breathed on them." This event takes place following the Savior's resurrection. The disciples had just gone through the dark period of the Savior's death, and now Jesus appeared to them and commissioned them to preach in Samaria, Galilee, and the world at large. They needed courage. He breathed new life into them the same way one might describe a team or business who gets a new member or manager. Someone reports, "He breathed new life into the team." Another says, "She's like a breath of fresh air." It is reported, "There seems to be a new air in the locker room."

We say these things today in our own language but are not able to easily associate the idioms from long ago with what we commonly say today. We "talk the talk," but do we "walk the walk"?

"eternal life"

This seems like a simple phrase. At first one would conclude that it means to have life eternally. However, eternal life is the promised reward of the most faithful. God has spoken, "And, if you keep my commandments and endure to the end you shall have **eternal life**, which gift is the greatest of all the gifts of God" (D&C 14:7; emphasis added).

However, you might ask, "do not all who are resurrected live forever?" The answer is in the affirmative. So the message of the idiom is not just in the words themselves, but in the message intended. "Eternal life" is the name of the kind of life that God lives.[4] In God's life he rules and has dominion. He has increase and his work is glorious and has to do with exaltation and glory. That is the message of "eternal life," not just living forever.

"burning bush"

What does a person mean if they say, "I can't help you. I've got too many irons in the fire?" The person likely means that he is too busy. But where does the meaning about too many irons in the fire come from and what does it mean? It's origin is found in the round up of cattle out on the range. Many open ranges contained cattle from various owners all mixed together. So to overcome the difficulty of each owner separating out his own cattle and branding all his new calves, they had a combined roundup. They simply all participated and when a calf was caught and identified as to its owner, then the owner's branding iron was taken out of the hot fire and used. The fire contained numerous irons and someone had to keep track of the various branding irons so as to not make a mistake and misbrand an animal. If this person made, or nearly made, a mistake, his response was, "I've got too many irons in the fire." You don't have to know all that in order to communicate that you are too busy. However, if someone new to the culture hasn't heard that expression or doesn't know the meaning of it, then he is prone to consider it as literal, but he'll get confused if he can't find your fire, let alone any irons.

Moses seeing a burning bush, which was not consumed, is just like that. The text reads, "And the angel of the Lord appeared unto him in a flame of fire out of the midst of a bush: and he looked, and, behold, the bush burned with fire, and the bush was not consumed" (Exodus 3:2). What is the message of a bush?

The people who lived during the time of the judges knew the meaning of a bush. They gave a name to a terrible ruler who killed all his brothers so that he could be the one to rule in Shechem. His name was Abimelech, but they called him "the bramble" or "the bush" because they were caught in the snare of his leadership. But this message of being caught in the "bush" or "bramble" is not totally removed from us. At least it is not if we remember the story about Brer Rabbit and Brer Bear and the bramble. Remember that Brer Bear didn't want to go into the bush after Brer Rabbit for fear that he would never come out. Well, the people made an alliance with Abimelech and they were caught by him, so they referred to him as "the bramble" (see Judges 9:14, 15).

Moses was told by God's messenger that the children of Israel were in a bush, or bramble, in Egypt. Of course Moses knew of their bondage because he was a product of their servitude. But Moses saw a flame of fire in the bush, which indicated that God was there and would be the source of their deliverance. This would be no more far-fetched than if you were in "hot water" or "up to your neck in alligators," and you phoned your rich uncle and asked him to "throw you a rope." Your wife asked you if you thought he would help you and you said you could "see a light at the end of the tunnel."

Using a burning bush as an idiom to indicate upcoming difficulties or being caught is no different than saying, "I can see nothing but storms ahead for us as a family. But I now can see a silver lining in all of this darkness." We speak of trouble and entanglements in many ways, such as, "There has been a cloud hanging over this project from the beginning." "Burning bush" should be read as an idiom just like "hot water." It is a descriptive expression of conditions as they were and as they were to become. It is figurative and not literal.

"sun stood still" "mine arm is lengthened"

Our words sometimes defy nature and science. They go beyond possibility. That is the very nature of hyperbole. We say, "When I first saw you, my heart just stopped still." Well, that did not happen, but this statement indicates the intensity and power of the moment. Or maybe "it rained cats and dogs." That would communicate the same idea. "When she comes into a room, time stands still." That of course tells a message regarding her beauty or presence and how it makes a difference to someone.

While conquering Canaan, Joshua records the following, "And the sun stood still, and the moon stayed, until the people had avenged themselves upon their enemies. Is not this written in the book of Jasher? So the **sun stood still** in the midst of heaven, and hasted not to go down about a whole day" (Joshua 10:13; emphasis added). The idea of this hyperbole was that even the universe shared in their battle for good and justified them in their cause.

Nephi made many prophecies regarding what God would do in the latter days. He warned those who rely on the "arm of flesh" and quoted the Lord using hyperbole, "For notwithstanding I shall lengthen out mine arm . . . if they will repent and come unto me; for **mine arm is lengthened** out all the day long, saith the Lord God of Hosts" (2 Nephi 28:32). The Lord's arm is not literally made longer. That is an idiom which tells that God's power is extended. For how long is his power extended? Just for a day? No! The whole expression is figurative. The whole message is about the unlimited mercy of God.

Interpreting hyperbole literally will distort and mislead us every time that we don't properly identify what we are reading. The prophet Habakkuk records a prayer and careful reading of the verses reveals the poetic nature of his prayer. Poetry is filled with figurative phrases. It seldom deals with the factual, but with intensities and emotions. His prayer is filled with idioms, one of which states, "The sun and moon stood still in their habitation: at the light of thine arrows they went, and at the shining of thy glittering spear" (Habakkuk 3:11).

To interpret Habakkuk's words literally would be a poor choice. The same kind of a poor choice as if one person says to another, "He was caught by the long arm of the law," or "When God closes a door to us, he always opens a window." These are metaphors that teach powerful concepts. They are not meant to be literal. Sometimes a person says, "I thought the day would never end. It just went on forever!" That surely is figurative and metaphoric! It tells feelings and does so in just a few words. "That was the longest day of my life" does not suggest a day with more than twenty-four hours. What it does, however, is say a lot about feelings and circumstances.

Mormon wrote his abridgement of the historical events of great wickedness among the Nephites. In his writing he spoke of the nothingness of men compared with the power of God. He attributed all things that happen, in and on the earth, as the result of the power of God. At first reading, one may conclude that God has lengthened out the day for hours at certain times for the benefit of man. However, careful reading of the chapter reveals that Mormon is speaking of the seasons and how the days are lengthened by hours. He speaks of the power of God that causes earthquakes and other seismic events. His summary is that if God has the power to do these things, then he can bless his people as well as withdraw blessings. Regarding the lengthening of days by seasons, he wrote, "Yea, if he say unto the earth—Thou shalt go back, that it lengthen out the day for many hours—it is done; And thus, according to his word the earth goeth back, and it appeareth unto man that the **sun standeth still**; yea, and behold, this is so; for surely it is the earth that moveth and not the sun" (Helaman 12:14–15; emphasis added).

This teaching by Mormon is not idiomatic. It is speaking of the actual change in the length of days in the seasons. It should not be used as evidence to show that Joshua's idiomatic statement has other testimonies that support a literal idea of "the sun standing still."

"mountain of the house of the Lord" "top of the mountains"

High places have always been the favorite locations for worship of Jehovah, but also for the false gods of Palestine and Canaan. During the times of David, there were altars on the high places of Jerusalem, Gilgal, Bethel, and Shechem. When disobedient kings, such as Solomon, David's son, placed idols and groves on these same locations, he was trying to satisfy his idolatress wives as well as the people who turned away from Jehovah. His motive was probably his attempt at being "politically correct." His attempt at political correctness is revealed in the scripture, "For they also built them high places, and images, and groves, on every high hill, and under every green tree" (1 Kings 14:23).

Altitude is not the issue in question. There are higher points or peaks surrounding Jerusalem other than Mount Moriah where Abraham was asked to offer Isaac as a sacrifice. The tabernacle used during the Israelites wandering in the wilderness was not pitched on high places, but among the people. But it was considered the highest place of worship at the time until it was permanently built as a temple on Mount Moriah. Regardless of the location of the place of worship, the words are used by the people, "Let us go up to the temple." It is more than a literal thing. When the first temple in the American west was built at St. George, it was literally a downward journey for almost everyone in the area. However, the sentiment of the Saints was always "Let us go up to the temple." It has never been, "Let us go down." Although, it is true that temples were built on hills in both Manti and Logan; the Salt Lake Temple and numerous other temples have been built in valleys, not on hillsides, or on mountains. There are, however, others that are elevated in their locations, but none have yet been built on the very top of a mountain.

Consider the words of Micah, "But in the last days it shall come to pass, that the **mountain of the house of the Lord** shall be established in the **top of the mountains**, and it shall be *exalted above the hills*; and people shall flow unto it" (Micah 4:1; emphasis added).

The Lord has clearly identified this verse as applying to Zion which is administered from the Salt Lake Valley. The Salt Lake Temple and all the facilities which surround it are referred to as the "Mountain of the Lord's House." However, this is an idiom. It is like saying that the Supreme Court is the highest court in the land. However, it is situated only a short elevation above sea level in Washington, DC. It is not literal but figurative.

In Micah's statement quoted above, notice that the mountain of the Lord would be exalted above the hills. Here the "hills" refer to all other worship. Compared to the mountain of the Lord, everything else only has the possibility of being hills. This figurative imagery continues in Micah's next verses:

> 2 And many nations shall come, and say, Come, and let us go up to the mountain of the Lord, and to the house of the God of Jacob; and he will teach us of his ways, and we will walk in his paths: for the law shall go forth of Zion, and the word of the Lord from Jerusalem.
>
> 3 And he shall judge among many people, and rebuke strong nations afar off; and they shall beat their swords into plowshares, and their spears into pruninghooks: nation shall not lift up a sword against nation, neither shall they learn war any more.

4 But they shall sit every man under his vine and under his fig tree; and none shall make them afraid: for the mouth of the Lord of hosts hath spoken it.

5 For all people will walk every one in the name of his god, and we will walk in the name of the Lord our God for ever and ever.

6 In that day, saith the Lord, will I assemble her that halteth, and I will gather her that is driven out, and her that I have afflicted;

7 And I will make her that halted a remnant, and her that was cast far off a strong nation: and the Lord shall reign over them in mount Zion from henceforth, even for ever, (Micah 4:2–7)

First of all, notice the figurative terms Micah uses. He uses "go up," "teach us of his ways," "walk in his paths," "law shall go forth of Zion," and the "word of the Lord from Jerusalem." Those are figurative terms just from verse 2. Consider all the others in the verses that follow.

So in conclusion: The "mountain of the Lord" is not so-called because it is the highest place. It is not at the "top of the mountains." Salt Lake City is in the valley whose elevation is lower than most cities in central and northern Utah as well as surrounding states. But the temple is a mountain, immovable, strong, and observable. It can be looked up to, and as you go there, you feel elevated, reaching toward God and his purposes. Isaiah, Nephi, Zechariah, and others used the same imagery in their declarations. We should understand their language just like our own today. We would understand if a sports team were said to be on top of the heap. Everyone else is trying to knock them off the top of the mountain where they have put themselves. This same kind of imagery has been used by the Lord and his prophets to influence our feelings and performance. These are idioms, not literal statements.

"remember them no more"

The word *remember* with its various forms of tense and sense, appears in the scriptures well over five hundred times. The definition for the word *remember* is not the same each time it is used. Like so many words, remember has multiple definitions. It can mean to:

a) recall,
b) keep in remembrance,
c) mention,
d) make a memorial, or
e) record.

A scriptural example of "recalling" would be, "Behold, you have been entrusted with these things, but how strict were your commandments; and **remember** also the promises which were made to you, if you did not transgress them" (D&C 3:5; emphasis added).

A scriptural example of "keeping in remembrance" would be, "And the children of Israel remembered not the Lord their God, who had delivered them out of the hands of all their enemies on every side" (Judges 8:34; emphasis added).

A scriptural example of "mentioning" would be: "And again, I say unto you, I **remember** my servant Oliver Granger; behold, verily I say unto him that his name shall be had in sacred **remembrance** from generation to generation, forever and ever, saith the Lord" (D&C 117:12; emphasis added).

A scriptural example of "making a memorial" would be, "And that these days should be **remembered** and kept throughout every generation, every family, every province, and every city; and that these days of Purim should not fail from among the Jews, nor the memorial of them perish from their seed" (Esther 9:28; emphasis added).

And lastly, a scriptural example of "recording" would be: "And it came to pass that the lawyers put it into their hearts that they should **remember** these things against him" (Alma 10:30; emphasis added).

With these various definitions and examples of the word *remember* in mind, we must determine which definition applies to the following verse. "Behold, he who has repented of his sins, the same is forgiven, and I, the Lord, **remember them no more**" (D&C 58:42; emphasis added).

If the word *remember* is defined here as a matter of recall, that would suggest that God, who is omniscient, does not have a good memory. That cannot be! Imagine praying to such a God and believing that he will not remember who we are or our circumstances and needs. It would preclude his atoning for our personal sins for he might only suffer for those individuals whom he remembers. God does not fail in recalling our sins. He knows how far the repentant have come and with what devotion they have yielded.

Some have felt that if they themselves cannot forget their sins, they have not been forgiven. This is not true! Both the Apostle Paul and Alma the Younger never forgot their past and how far they were into rebellion. They both spoke of the sweetness of forgiveness.

The message of the idiom "remembered them no more," cited above, is that our repented sins will no longer be recorded. They need not be dealt with again. The idea that God has swept them from his memory is not doctrinally sound. If we do something for someone and they want to repay us, it is often the case that we say, "Oh, just forget it." That does not suggest for them to have a poor memory. However, the message is that it is not recorded or on the ledger needing repayment. There are many instances in scripture wherein we can identify this same message as the word *remember* is used. The Lord said, "Verily I say unto you, notwithstanding their sins, my bowels are filled with compassion towards them. I will not utterly cast them off; and in the day of wrath I will remember mercy" (D&C 101:9). When messages of remembering are considered, if they are not about the subject of recall, they should be considered as likely having figurative or idiomatic interpretations.

"chains of hell"

What conditions could involve something so terrible? Chains seem so controlling and unbreakable. Is this idiom describing a condition of mortality or one of eternity? Father Lehi, when near the end of his mortal life, spoke prophetically to future generations of descendants who would possess the land to which he had immigrated. He said, "O that ye would awake; awake from a deep sleep, yea, even from the **sleep of hell**, and shake off the awful **chains** by which ye are bound, which are the **chains** which bind the children of men, that they are carried away captive down to the eternal gulf of misery and woe" (2 Nephi 1:13; emphasis added).

Alma told of his heritage to the people of Zarahemla. He rehearsed how his father had been converted and then how his father had converted others who then freed themselves from the false doctrines of wicked leaders and were helped by God to join the people of Zarahemla. Alma recounted what his father had done. "Behold, he changed their hearts; yea, he awakened them out of a deep sleep, and they awoke unto God. Behold, they were in the midst of darkness; nevertheless, their souls were illuminated by the light of the everlasting word; yea, they were encircled about by the bands of death, and the **chains of hell**, and an everlasting destruction did await them" (Alma 5:7; emphasis added). He continued, "And again I ask, were the bands of death broken, and the **chains of hell** which encircled them about, were they loosed? I say unto you, Yea, they were loosed, and their souls did expand, and they did sing redeeming love. And I say unto you that they are saved" (Alma 5:9; emphasis added).

The final fate of the wicked as being bound with chains and being in hell is rather an expected outcome for those who have followed Satan. However, both Lehi and Alma encouraged wakening out of sleep while in mortality and becoming free from the "chains of hell." Fortunately, Alma supplies the definition for this idiom that applies to both conditions, which can be broken in this mortal life as well as a final outcome for the wicked. He said: "And they that will harden their hearts, to them is given the lesser portion of the word until they know nothing concerning his mysteries; and then they are taken captive by the devil, and led by his will down to destruction. Now this is what is meant by the **chains of hell**" (Alma 12:11; emphasis added).

So a process is involved with becoming chained. It happens in mortality and has to do with hardening our hearts and becoming ignorant of the mysteries of God. In mortality, we begin to experience the chains as we harden our feelings. The best scriptural definition or synonym for "heart" is "feelings." So if we harden our hearts, we become less sensitive to feelings. When we do that, the chains of hell are controlling us. Other relevant verses containing the idiom are Alma 13:30; Alma 26:14; Doctrine and Covenants 123:8; Doctrine and Covenants 138:23; 2 Peter 2:4; 2 Nephi 28:22.

"rise up quickly"

The story of Peter in prison, chained between two soldiers, seems to take on a feeling of intrigue and urgency, when the record states that the angel told Peter to "rise up quickly." Without understanding the idiom used, the reader feels that Peter must move with haste or he will be caught by the guards, either those beside him or those posted at the prison entrance. Generally we think Peter was to not be slow in his rising up. The word *quick* is generally interpreted this way by Westerners as dealing with time. However, we should think of him going forward with life and power. Peter is told to rise because the power of God is with him. He is with an angel who has the power to free him from chains and anything else that resisted them. Why should they have to hurry? Consider the following verses regarding the quick and the dead.

They speak of those that are alive (quick) and those that are dead.

- And now I bid unto all, farewell. I soon go to rest in the paradise of God, until my spirit and body shall again reunite, and I am brought forth triumphant through the air, to meet you before the pleasing bar of the great Jehovah, the Eternal Judge of both **quick and dead**. Amen (Moroni 10:34; emphasis added).
- And he commanded us to preach unto the people, and to testify that it is he which was ordained of God to be the Judge of **quick and dead**. (Acts 10:42; emphasis added).
- I charge thee therefore before God, and the Lord Jesus Christ, who shall judge the **quick and the dead** at his appearing and his kingdom. (2 Timothy 4:1; emphasis added).
- Who shall give account to him that is ready to judge the **quick and the dead**. (1 Peter 4:5; emphasis added)

"I come quickly"

Another idiom uses the same word and requires the same definition of the words *quick* or *quickly*. Fifteen times in scripture the Lord says: "I come quickly." Likely the most known of these statements is recorded in the Book of Revelation almost two thousand years ago. The Lord said, "Behold, I come quickly: blessed is he that keepeth the sayings of the prophecy of this book" (Revelation 22:7). The oft-asked question is, "Why did God say that so long ago, and still he hasn't come again?" The answer is already given. *Quickly* means with life and power. Both life and power are included in the Lord's statement: "And behold, and lo, I come quickly to judgment, to convince all of their ungodly deeds which they have committed against me, as it is written of me in the volume of the book" (D&C 99:5).

This understanding of the meaning of the word *quickly* turns this saying which creates doubt to one of grandeur and magnitude. "I come quickly" means that God will come with life. Some will recognize our present idiom regarding the pain involved when we say, "I cut myself clear to the quick." That means that we cut ourselves deep enough to get into the nerves and it hurt. Figuratively we speak also of the same phenomenon relative to emotional pain. It is often said, "She's got one sharp tongue. She sliced me up real bad. She cut me clear to the quick."

"thou shalt not forswear thyself"

Many scriptural words are unfamiliar to us in our language. We no longer use them. Such a word is "forswear." Jesus taught:

> 33 Again, ye have heard that it hath been said by them of old time, **Thou shalt not forswear thyself**, but shalt perform unto the Lord thine oaths:
>
> 34 But I say unto you, Swear not at all; neither by heaven; for it is God's throne:
>
> 35 Nor by the earth; for it is his footstool: neither by Jerusalem; for it is the city of the great King.
>
> 36 Neither shalt thou swear by thy head, because thou canst not make one hair white or black.
>
> 37 But let your communication be, Yea, yea; Nay, nay: for whatsoever is more than these cometh of evil. (Matthew 5:33–37; emphasis added)

Because of what the Savior taught in verse 37, many have concluded that we should never swear or make promises. This, however, is where the definition of forswear comes into play. *Forswear* means to swear beyond our time or ability to fulfill. Verse 36 illustrates things that cannot be changed. So don't swear or promise to make such things come about. It was thought by some that if you would swear by something living, your sworn word was certain to take place or become true. That is the reason heaven, the earth, and Jerusalem are illustrated in verses 34 and 35. They are very living things.

Thus, all these principles spoken of by the Savior in verses 33 through 36 are about forswearing. But in verse 37, the Savior tells us how we should perform. We should only swear to do things that are within our power. That is swearing, not forswearing. We should not forswear.

"unforgivable sin"

This phrase as an idiom should be rather transparent. However, it is often misunderstood because of the definition of the word *forgive*. If you have done something to me and I say, "I forgive you" technically, that is not a proper use of the word because forgive suggests that benevolence has already occurred. Other words like it are *forewarn*, *foresee*, *forethought*. They all tell of things before they happen. Like these words just mentioned, it is the prefix of *forgive* that tells its tense. As an example, a golfer calls out "fore" to warn other golfers ahead of him that he has hit a ball improperly. It is out of his control, because he has already hit it. Forgive indicates mercy that has already been given. The prefix "fore" means before and "give" means imparting or granting.

In the Sermon on the Mount, the Savior teaches about prayer, "And forgive us our debts, as we forgive our debtors" (Matthew 6:12). He did not instruct us to plead with Heavenly Father to pardon us, but to forgive us. A pardon is granting or conferring after the act has been done. Forgiveness is in action even before the act is committed. Furthermore, we were given from the councils held before this life even began, the oath and promise from God our Eternal Father that he would provide a Savior, who would suffer for our sins if we would forsake them. That is forgiveness!

We are required to have this attitude and mind-set that God has. "I, the Lord, will forgive whom I will forgive, but of you it is required to forgive all men" (D&C 64:10). The command is stated in another way: "For, if ye forgive men their trespasses your heavenly Father will also forgive you; But if ye forgive not men their trespasses neither will your Father forgive your trespasses" (3 Nephi 13:14–15).

This proper definition helps us as we read from "The Law" of the Church, revealed in 1831:

> 18 And now, behold, I speak unto the church. Thou shalt not kill; and **he that kills shall not have forgiveness** in this world, nor in the world to come.
>
> 19 And again, I say, thou shalt not kill; but he that killeth shall die.
>
> 20 Thou shalt not steal; and he that stealeth and will not repent shall be cast out.
>
> 21 Thou shalt not lie; he that lieth and will not repent shall be cast out.
>
> 22 Thou shalt love thy wife with all thy heart, and shalt cleave unto her and none else.
>
> 23 And he that looketh upon a woman to lust after her shall deny the faith, and shall not have the Spirit; and if he repents not he shall be cast out.
>
> 24 Thou shalt not commit adultery; and he that committeth adultery, and repenteth not, shall be cast out.
>
> 25 But he that has committed adultery and repents with all his heart, and forsaketh it, and doeth it no more, thou shalt forgive;

26 But if he doeth it again, **he shall not be forgiven**, but shall be cast out. (D&C 42:18–26; emphasis added)

These verses make clear the following:

a) Killing (murder) is an unforgivable sin (verse 18)
b) He that killeth (murders) shall die (verse 19)
c) To steal (verse 20); to lie (verse 21); to look upon another woman who is not your wife (verse 23); and to commit adultery (verse 24); shall be forgiven if there is true repentance.
d) If one has been forgiven of adultery, and it is done again, they shall not be forgiven, but cast out of the Church (verse 26).

So all sins, if repented of, with the exception of murder, shall be forgiven. Therefore, murder is the "unforgivable sin"! But the question surfaces: "What about the person who commits adultery, repents, then does it again?" The law says that he shall not be forgiven! That is true. He shall not be forgiven, but must seek a pardon, from God, which can come after the fact—he is not forgiven because forgiveness no longer applies! Such a person—for this sin—must "go into the depths of hell" themselves and pay the price. Then he must seek and hope for a pardon from God. Ideally, this pardon can be attained while in mortality. Many see verse 26 as holding out no hope for them, but there is! For them there is not forgiveness, but there can be a pardon. God intends to save us all, and even those who commit the unforgivable sin have hope. They have not committed the "unpardonable sin." Even David, who committed adultery with Bathsheba and then had her husband Uriah killed, expressed hope of a pardon, but not forgiveness. Such a pardon for murder will not come in this life. Murderers cannot join the Church by baptism. After they have paid the full penalty for their crime, they inherit the telestial kingdom, which is a kingdom of glory.

"unpardonable sin"

If all sins, except shedding innocent blood, can be forgiven, and even those who do shed innocent blood have a chance for a pardon, what does that leave? There is an act which is unpardonable. What is this sin?

"All sins shall be forgiven, except the sin against the Holy Ghost; for Jesus will save all except the sons of perdition. What must a man do to commit the unpardonable sin? He must receive the Holy Ghost, have the heavens opened unto him, and know God, and then sin against him. After a man has sinned against the Holy Ghost, there is no repentance for him. He has got to say that the sun does not shine while he sees it; he has got to deny Jesus Christ when the heavens have been opened unto him, and to deny the plan of salvation with his eyes open to the truth of it; and from that time he begins to be an enemy. This is the case with many apostates of the Church of Jesus Christ of Latter-day Saints."[5]

Elder Bruce R. McConkie made the following statement regarding the unpardonable sin: "He thereby commits murder by assenting unto the Lord's death, that is, having a perfect knowledge of the truth he comes out in open rebellion and places himself in a position wherein he would have crucified Christ knowing perfectly the while that he was the Son of God. Christ is thus crucified afresh and put to open shame."[6]

It is essential that we understand both the "unforgivable sin" and the "unpardonable sin." If we do so, we will see the great plan of the Father and not lose hope because we have sinned, no matter the horribleness of the transgression. We will know that there is only one act that puts us beyond God's mercy. The only decision I must make is if I want to suffer for sin myself or if I want to be the benefactor of the Savior's suffering for me. He has already done so. That is forgiveness. If I refuse to repent, then there still must be an atonement for my sins. It will be made by me and is not covered by the payment made long ago by the Savior.

"blood of the covenant"
Exodus 24:8; Zechariah 9:11; Hebrews 10:27; 13:20

In our world today we make covenants and contracts all the time. They are agreements between parties. Our covenants today are evidenced by documents, signed and generally witnesses or notarized. If anyone challenges the covenant, we have an original or a copy of the original as evidence and a statement of the covenant conditions. These covenants can be made between people in one another's presence or can be made while separated by thousands of miles. In a world with little ability to record and store such transactions, making covenants employed other means. Covenants made in biblical times involved monuments, blood, scars, and other emblems, which could not be duplicated. As Westerners, we seem to not understand or respect the seriousness of covenants. If an agreement gets inconvenient or boring, we simply get out of it. Consider today's disastrous divorce rates, bankruptcies, and apathy for religious ordinances. Adam was commanded to offer blood sacrifice:

> 5 And he gave unto them commandments, that they should worship the Lord their God, and should offer the firstlings of their flocks, for an offering unto the Lord. And Adam was obedient unto the commandments of the Lord.
>
> 6 And after many days an angel of the Lord appeared unto Adam, saying: Why dost thou offer sacrifices unto the Lord? And Adam said unto him: I know not, save the Lord commanded me.
>
> 7 And then the angel spake, saying: This thing is a similitude of the sacrifice of the Only Begotten of the Father, which is full of grace and truth. (Moses 5:5–7)

The blood sacrifice was not the covenant but was the testimony of the covenant. It was a covenant between our Father in Heaven and us as his children. We learn from other scriptural details of the sacrifice that the blood was caught in a basin or a cupped hand and placed on the altar or on the sacrifices in prescribed places. On occasions it was sprinkled on the people participating as a group in the covenant, sprinkled or poured on the altar, or placed on a memorial such as a rock or tree, or on the bodies of those participating in the sacrifice (see Exodus 24:6–8, Leviticus 6:27, 8:24; Hebrews 9:19–21).

The blood of the covenant makers was sometimes mingled by cutting the flesh of both participants in the same location and holding the wounds together. Some give this as the origin for the handshake or grasp between covenant makers. The Hebrew word for covenant is *berith*, and one of its definitions is "to cut until blood flows." Today some put great significance upon the consummating a deal with a handshake. They seem to feel it is even more binding than a legal document. These ideas regarding the significance of a handshake possibly should be more paramount as we consider them as the pattern taught by covenants of blood. Another definition for *berith* is covenant or testament. Mingling of blood could also be accomplished by putting blood into wine and drinking it, even though drinking the blood itself was forbidden. The purpose of mingling the blood with something like wine is the symbolic or actual idea of taking part of the other partner into your life—to make them a part of you and to make you more like them.

The wound made from which the blood flowed could be filled with a material so that a scar would develop or the blood would remain on the memorial, both as a testimony and reminder to the parties of their covenant rights and responsibilities. Sometimes a new tree was planted or a stone was erected and given a name while blood was placed upon it. When such a blood covenant was made, it was considered the most sacred of all contracts. When you enter into a blood covenant with someone, you promise to give him or her your life, your devotion to their needs, and your total respect.

When blood is mingled, it suggests the taking on of the characteristics of the other party. The parties would exchange names as a means of becoming like each other. Since they were known by each other's names they would be expected to think, act, and talk like their blood-covenant partner. Even clothing and possessions could be exchanged to assist in the process.

A memorial meal to symbolize their covenant union was served. They would take a loaf of bread and break it in two and feed it to each other. Then they could serve each other wine. These emblems represented their lives. By exchanging them, the two parties express their desire to become part of each other.

It should not be difficult to match these details of the blood sacrifice with the great plan of our Father in Heaven from the very beginning to the present. We can identify:

The Sacrifice	Jesus Christ, God's Only Begotten Son in the flesh
Blood Sprinkled	"And Moses took the blood, and sprinkled it on the people, and said, Behold the blood of the covenant, which the Lord hath made with you concerning all these words" (Exodus 24:8).
Blood on memorial	Christ's blood was on a tree (the cross) (Exodus 24:6)
Cutting till blood flowed	Jesus' hands, wrists, side
Scar	Marks in Jesus' side, hands, and feet (3 Nephi 11:14; D&C 6:37)

Sacrifice of Jesus' life	To keep his part of covenant—the same as we should be willing to do with our own (Mosiah 5:8)
Hand grasp	Mingling our blood with his
The name of Christ	We take upon us the name of Christ—he takes upon himself our sins and suffers for them (D&C 20:37).
He is a man of sorrows	Christ knows our needs and gives us accordingly
Memorial supper	The sacrament—we eat and drink emblems of him—we take him into our lives. If we become like him, we can have his spirit to be with us

Before his coming as the Mortal Messiah, sacrifice was offered as a testimony of what he would do for us all. Since his offering, we have scars, a name, and a memorial, all of which testify that Heavenly Father kept his part of the covenant. Our part of the covenant should be kept even at the peril of our own lives.

Understanding these concepts of a covenant of blood helps us understand some cloudy scriptural events such as when Zipporah did what Moses had covenanted to do, but had not done.

"And the Lord spared Moses and let him go, because Zipporah, his wife, circumcised the child. And she said, Thou art a bloody husband. And Moses was ashamed, and hid his face from the Lord, and said, I have sinned before the Lord" (JST Exodus 4:26).

At first reading it may seem she is cursing her husband, Moses, but in light of the covenant of blood, it reads more like an admonition. Zipporah was reminding Moses that he is a covenant man of God and she is intent on helping him keep his part of the agreement.

The concepts of the covenant of blood also give insight into the relationship of David and Jonathan, the son of King Saul. Jonathan knew that his father had been rejected by the Lord as king. As Saul's oldest son, Jonathan would have been the next king, but he knew that David had been anointed by Samuel to reign instead of his father. Yet he supported David, saved his life, and was someone David could trust. They did some things which some wonder about. They exchanged garments and weapons (1 Samuel 18:1–4). Knowing that this was a part of the covenant they had made with each other answers why they did such things.

Abraham's determination to do as God commanded and offer his birthright son as a sacrifice takes on new meaning because of the blood of the covenant. Abraham was fully determined to offer Isaac (Genesis 22:9–13). He was at the point of raising the knife when he was restrained by the Lord and shown the ram caught in the nearby thicket. Our natural feelings cry out, and we say that we could not do such a thing as Abraham was about to do. But the element of a covenant of blood required such, and Abraham and Isaac both determined to fulfill their end of the covenant. The same emotions are present in reading of Jesus' determination to fulfill his part of the covenant of blood on behalf of us all (see D&C 19:18–20). Our present day attitude regarding keeping covenants insinuates that surely it would not be necessary to carry out the act. However, that is the principle of a covenant of blood. It is binding, and we must keep our part of the agreement.

When the disobedient Israelites, newly freed from Egypt, sinned while Moses was long on the mountain, and they lost faith in God's deliverance, Moses seems to bargain with the Lord on behalf of them all. Moses says, "Yet now, if thou wilt forgive their sin—; and if not, blot me, I pray thee, out of thy book which thou hast written" (Exodus 32:32). Applying the covenant of blood principles, Moses expects that his life should be shed because of his lack of performance in getting the people ready to follow him to the promised land.

It seemed significant that on many occasions that Jehovah was given a new name. The significance of a new name for God is lost in the story unless the principles of a covenant of blood are applied. David calls his blood partner *Jehovah-Raah*, which means "the Lord, my shepherd or friend." To Abraham, God is called *Jehovah-Jireh*, which the Lord is my provider (Genesis 22:14). God had provided the ram in the thicket. When the Israelites defeated the Amalekites in battle, God was called *Jehovah-Nissi*, the Lord is my banner in victory (Exodus 17:15). The Law given at Mt. Sinai was intended to make the people a holy nation, one set apart from all other peoples of the earth. God became known as *Jehovah-Meloddishken*, "the Lord who sanctifies or sets you apart." In the dark hours of Israel's history, *Jehovah-Shalom*, the Lord is peace, revealed himself to Gideon (Judges 6:24). Provoked by her rival, barren Hannah entreated *Jehovah-Sabaoth*, the Lord of hosts (delivery) to give her a child. Jeremiah described the coming messiah as *Jehovah-Tsid-kenu*, the Lord of righteousness.

When individuals have made a covenant with God, there is a record of some of their newly given names; e.g. Abram to Abraham, Sarai to Sarah, Jacob to Israel, Saul to Paul, and Simon to Cephas or Peter. A new name is an indication that a covenant of the blood was made and a new life of taking on the character traits of the covenant partner was set in motion. Our modern practice of the wife taking on herself the name of her husband is generally lost in other customs and traditions. However, this process should be clearly seen as a pattern of a blood covenant. If properly carried out, celestial marriage will not take place until the groom has taken upon himself the name of Melchizedek, whose name was "King of Righteousness" (see footnote a, Genesis 14:18). Therefore, both parties making the covenant have followed this pattern. Furthermore, the wedding cake, along with a traditional drink, fit the idea of "breaking bread" or having a "memorial meal" together. So if we can "get the hang of things" and "cut through all the red tape," we can see that "these things are not to be sneezed at." The "covenant of blood" was not just something bloody and from the past—it is beautiful and still alive today!

Notes

1. Bruce R. McConkie, *A New Witness for the Articles of Faith*, (Salt Lake City: Deseret Book, 1980), 59.
2. See George M. Peacock, *Unlocking the Numbers*, (Springville, Utah: Cedar Fort, 2005), 22.
3. George M. Lamsa, *Gospel Light* (San Francisco: Holman, 1939), 37.
4. See Bruce R. McConkie, "The Ten Blessings of Priesthood," *Ensign*, Nov. 1977, 34.
5. Joseph Fielding Smith, *Teachings of the Prophet Joseph Smith*, (Salt Lake City: Deseret Book, 1977), 358.
6. Bruce R. McConkie, *Mormon Doctrine*, (Salt Lake City: Bookcraft, 1958), 3:161.

IDIOMS REGARDING THE ATONEMENT

"to cover"

While the subject of the Atonement is central to all of the writings of the New Testament, the word *atonement* is almost non-existent in that volume of scripture. When one tries to answer the question of why that is so, understanding the word and its equivalent synonyms can be so helpful. The first thing to know is that the word *atonement* is an English word. Dictionaries generally define the word as "reconciliation," or "satisfaction for." It can also be defined as reparation for an offense or injury. It is unique to the English language. What does that mean? It means that there is no equivalent word in the Bible languages that means the same as it does. It cannot be translated from English to Aramaic, Hebrew, or Greek with one equivalent word. So, even though the Bible speaks abundantly on the Atonement, seldom does the word appear in our present English texts. You may ask, "Are there other words that come close to being the equivalent of the word *atonement*, and if so, what are they?" The answer is yes and the best equivalent word in Hebrew is *kaphar* which means "to cover." If we look for the expressions of "to cover" or "covering" and their opposites, we can find a plethora of writings regarding the Atonement. Some examples from both the Old and the New Testament follow. However, instead of being one word instances they will be phrases which are idiomatic.

Peter wrote: "And above all things have fervent charity among yourselves: for charity **shall cover** the multitude of sins" (1 Peter 4:8; emphasis added). He stated that if we have the "pure love of Christ" (charity) that devotion to Christ will cover (atone for) a multitude of sins. Sometimes this teaching of Peter leads us down the wrong path when the word *charity* is defined as simply giving to the needy. Many contributions have been given by wealthy people in hopes that such charity would bring forgiveness of sins. However, forgiveness of sins comes from conduct that goes far beyond simply the giving of goods. It comes from contrition and true repentance or change. Without such change, we are in a position such as mentioned by Isaiah wherein he said to the unrepentant of his day, "Woe to the rebellious children, saith the Lord, that take counsel, but not of me; and that **cover with a covering**, but not of my spirit, that they may add sin to sin" (Isaiah 30:1; emphasis added). He spoke for God and said, to those unrepentant souls, that if they took counsel that was not from him, that they were being covered by an atonement that was not sanctioned by God's spirit. Because such action was not true, they were adding sin to their previous sin. Understanding what he was meaning when we read the word *cover* helps understand his message.

Elder Russell M. Nelson spoke regarding the words *atonement* and *cover* in general conference. He said: "Rich meaning is found in study of the word *atonement* in the Semitic languages of the Old Testament times. In Hebrew, the basic word for atonement is *kaphar*, a word that means 'to cover' or 'to forgive.' "[1]

"they were naked"

If we are not covered, then another idiomatic phrase comes into play. It is so descriptive of not being covered. It is the condition of being "naked." When Moses returned to the people after being absent from them and on the mountain receiving revelation from God, the people had reverted to their sins of idiolatry. Therefore the account tells, "And when Moses saw that the people **were naked**; (for Aaron had made them **naked** unto their shame among their enemies)" (Exodus 32:25; emphasis added). The account is not referring to a lack of clothing, but of sin and therefore not being covered by God because they had not repented.

When King Ahaz led the Kingdom of Judah toward evil and wickedness, the written accounts states, "For the Lord brought Judah low because of Ahaz king of Israel [should be Judah]; for he made Judah

naked, and transgressed sore against the Lord" (2 Chronicles 28:19; emphasis added). The idiom of being naked is not to be taken literally, but as a sign of an unrepentant state. Knowing that the word *naked* meant "unforgiven," rather than "having no clothing," adds clarity to the story.

Both of these words, *covered* and *naked*, are used by Job to describe hell. He wrote, "Hell is **naked** before him, and destruction hath no **covering**" (Job 26:6; emphasis added). If there is a place that is not covered by the atoning work of the Savior, it is hell, for hell is the abode of those that are unrepentant and still filthy. They must suffer themselves for their sins (see D&C 76:102–106).

Nephi made it clear that nakedness had to do with sin from which we had not turned. He wrote, "Wherefore, we shall have a perfect knowledge of all our guilt, and our uncleanness, and our **nakedness**; and the righteous shall have a perfect knowledge of their enjoyment, and their righteousness, being **clothed with purity**, yea, even with the robe of righteousness" (2 Nephi 9:14; emphasis added).

With an understanding of the words *naked* and *covered*, the account in the Garden of Eden takes on much more meaning, or possibly new meaning.

Chapter two of Genesis closes with the following words that include the word *naked*. Is it literal or figurative? Is it both? Which would be the more important message or have the greater consequence? Ask yourself as you read the verse. "And they were both naked, the man and his wife, and were not ashamed" (Genesis 2:25). If they were the only two living, and the only two of their gender which existed, as well as haven been given to one another in the previous verse, what is the purpose of clothing? They had not committed sin therefore, there was no reason for shame. However, in chapter three of Genesis, they disobey God's commands and Adam said to God that he was afraid, because he was naked, and that he hid himself. If his nakedness was literal, and he had felt no shame with God's previous visits, what changed after he partook of the fruit? The account in chapter three reads:

> 1 Now the serpent was more subtil than any beast of the field which the Lord God had made. And he said unto the woman, Yea, hath God said, Ye shall not eat of every tree of the garden?
>
> 2 And the woman said unto the serpent, We may eat of the fruit of the trees of the garden:

3 But of the fruit of the tree which is in the midst of the garden, God hath said, Ye shall not eat of it, neither shall ye touch it, lest ye die.

4 And the serpent said unto the woman, Ye shall not surely die:

5 For God doth know that in the day ye eat thereof, then your eyes shall be opened, and ye shall be as gods, knowing good and evil.

6 And when the woman saw that the tree [was] good for food, and that it was pleasant to the eyes, and a tree to be desired to make one wise, she took of the fruit thereof, and did eat, and gave also unto her husband with her; and he did eat.

7 And the eyes of them both were opened, and **they knew that they were naked**; and they sewed fig leaves together, and made themselves aprons.

8 And they heard the voice of the Lord God walking in the garden in the cool of the day: and Adam and his wife hid themselves from the presence of the Lord God amongst the trees of the garden.

9 And the Lord God called unto Adam, and said unto him, Where art thou?

10 And he said, I heard thy voice in the garden, and I was afraid, **because I was naked**; and I hid myself.

11 And he said, Who told thee **that thou wast naked**? Hast thou eaten of the tree, whereof I commanded thee that thou shouldest not eat?

12 And the man said, The woman whom thou gavest to be with me, she gave me of the tree, and I did eat.

13 And the Lord God said unto the woman, What is this that thou hast done? And the woman said, The serpent beguiled me, and I did eat.

14 And the Lord God said unto the serpent, Because thou hast done this, thou art cursed above all cattle, and above every beast of the field; upon thy belly shalt thou go, and dust shalt thou eat all the days of thy life:

15 And I will put enmity between thee and the woman, and between thy seed and her seed; it shall bruise thy head, and thou shalt bruise his heel.

16 Unto the woman he said, I will greatly multiply thy sorrow and thy conception; in sorrow thou shalt bring forth children; and thy desire shall be to thy husband, and he shall rule over thee.

17 And unto Adam he said, Because thou hast hearkened unto the voice of thy wife, and hast eaten of the tree, of which I commanded thee, saying, Thou shalt not eat of it: cursed is the ground for thy sake; in sorrow shalt thou eat of it all the days of thy life;

18 Thorns also and thistles shall it bring forth to thee; and thou shalt eat the herb of the field;

19 In the sweat of thy face shalt thou eat bread, till thou return unto the ground; for out of it wast thou taken: for dust thou [art], and unto dust shalt thou return.

20 And Adam called his wife's name Eve; because she was the mother of all living.

21 Unto Adam also and to his wife did the Lord God make coats of skins, **and clothed them**. (Genesis 3:1–21; emphasis added). (Reading the coinciding account in Moses 4:5–27 adds additional information to the Genesis verses.)

The next idiom gives the answer to the questions asked prior to the quotation of the verses.

"clothed them"

Words which are opposite of the meaning or terms you are considering, will often assist your understanding. So, while looking for the word *naked* in the account cited previously, do not overlook the word *clothed* in the last verse. God gives something to Adam and Eve that they need because they have disobeyed his commands. Genesis 3:21 states, "Unto Adam also and to his wife did the Lord God make coats of skins, and clothed them." When God gave them garments to cover their nakedness to which reference is made therein, the statement "and clothed them" may have reference to something far more significant than to articles of clothing.

To say that a man and his wife walk through life side by side, means far more than the position they take as they walk. It means that they are in harmony, equal, and facing the journeys of life together. They may actually walk by the side of each other, but the idiom "side by side" means much more. This same dualism can be applied to "wearing rings" and "leaving father and mother." When a mother asks her unmarried daughter, "Are you sleeping with that man?" She is not asking about sleep. In the same manner of speech, God is speaking about the Atonement to Adam and Eve and for all who will be born as their descendants. The clothing, even though it is meant to cover them, it will only partially do so, whereas the covering of the Atonement will completely, totally, and thoroughly shield them from the affects of sin. The skins of animals slain and the garment given as a covering are only symbolic of what really took place.

Regarding this connection between the idea of being clothed and the doctrine of the Atonement being taught to Adam and Eve, Joseph F. McConkie describes the beauty of the symbolism regarding the skins from which God made them clothing. He and others suggest that the covering was most likely made from the animals which Adam offered as his first sacrifice.[2]

This animal sacrifice was offered in the similitude of the offering of God's only begotten Son—the Savior of the world, who would come to earth as a man, born of a virgin, in the meridian of time, and be sacrificed for the redemption of God's children. This atoning sacrifice would break both the bonds of death as well as pay for the sins of all mankind. Adam and Eve were given this clothing, and it was a constant reminder of the greatest of all elements performed in mortality—the Atonement of Jesus our Savior. The wearing of the garment given to Adam and Eve would be a constant reminder and would permeate their lives and be a constant guiding influence. Endowed Latter-day Saints look at this symbolism as a present-day symbol rather than just a Garden of Eden experience. This gives another reason for "clothed" or "clothing" to be considered as an idiom full of meaning beyond the actual words.

If we only look for and only find the literal messages that are in the scriptures, we likely will look for the literal in all messages and actions within real life. The figurative is the language of the "romantics," and the "lovers." They thrive on poetry and music. The figurative is experienced in the bedtime stories read by parents to children and is replayed over and over again at Fairyland or the Magic Kingdom. If parents only attend such places for the rides and not the fantasy, they should get in for only half price. Scripture reading is the same. We must see more than just the literal, for God gives figurative instructions, which, if obeyed, will teach us saving truths. Abraham evidently did not see the figurative at first in God's command for him to sacrifice his son Isaac. It wasn't until he heard the voice restraining him and seeing the ram caught in the thicket. Eve did not literally die when she partook of the forbidden fruit. Eve was speaking to Satan in the Garden of Eden, not to a literal snake. When Eve's "eyes were opened," that does not mean that she had no eyesight before that time.

So the messages of clothing and being clothed are about the Atonement of Christ. The instructions given in the Garden of Eden and in the temple, regarding being clothed, should be read while expecting disclosures of truth and splendor that go far beyond the literal words and actions. Adam and Eve may not have had clothing at first in the garden, and were therefore naked. However, the word *naked* is about something far more important. Their actual clothing was likely a reminder of their being covered just as partaking emblems of our Lord's flesh and blood help us remember his sacrifice. We do not have to actually eat those emblems in order to remember his sacrifice; however, by so doing, it is more likely for us to remember and appreciate God's sacrifice for us. So, if we think of Adam and Eve without clothing of any kind while in the Garden, that is acceptable, however we should know that something greater is spoken of when their nakedness is reported.

"upon thy belly shalt thou go" "dust shalt thou eat"

Satan is told that he would eat dust all the days of his life. There is a similar message if a woman tells a man that she is going to make him "crawl" to ever get her approval again. Some seeking approval are told to "lick my boots." Or one race driver tells another that he is going to make him "eat dust" during the race, even though the race is being held on pavement. All these are idioms. They are figurative expressions that tell far more than the literal words. The woman wants the man to come to her and act like a man and apologize for whatever caused her anger and ire. The man licking the boots is not literally doing so, but he is indicating that he will do anything, anything at all, even something as humbling himself to such an action. Likewise, the drivers challenge one another and use expressions from the cattle trail, where no one wanted to "bring up the rear" and have to "eat dust" all day long. This "eating dust" would be opposed to being up front in fresh air and leading the herd to good pasture and water. Lucifer was told that he would never act like a man nor lead others where they should go and that there was great reason for shame.

Recognizing that idioms are used to tell more than the words themselves is always enlightening. A person might say, "My father would roll over in his grave if he knew what I had done." There is no way that could be taken literally, but, oh, the feeling that is generated by the idiom. It is enormous and moving. I have a "fire in my belly" for such learning!

"buried with him in baptism"

The concept of a covering being equated with the Atonement raises other questions. The questions reach into doctrines and ordinances, which have meanings sometimes undisclosed. The ordinance of baptism is associated so often with a washing away of sins that the concept of a covering is seldom considered. Ordinances often have more than one symbol associated with them and the washing symbol is beautiful and suggestive. However, at every baptism, two witnesses are in place to attest that the ordinance was performed properly and that the candidate was totally immersed or covered. They are not witnesses to see that a washing took place, but that there was a covering. Little children under the age of eight are under God's mercy and need no baptism (see Moroni 8:11–20), but those who are older and in need of repentance, are covered for the remission of their sins. Therefore, they need to take upon them the name of the Savior and the ordinance for so doing is being covered in the waters of baptism. Paul wrote that we were buried with the Lord in baptism which suggests being covered as well as rising from the water or grave with a newness of life. "Therefore we are buried with him by baptism into death: that like as Christ was raised up from the dead by the glory of the Father, even so we also should walk in newness of life" (Romans 6:4).

Paul wrote corresponding words to another group of saints. He communicated: "Buried with him in baptism, wherein also ye are risen with him through the faith of the operation of God, who hath raised him from the dead" (Colossians 2:12).

"as a hen gathereth her chickens under her wings"

In addition to being covered as individuals, Jesus spoke of covering numerous people by his Atonement. He does not use the word *cover*. However, for those who have watched the process of a mother hen putting numerous little chicks under her wings, amazement is generally the result. The amazement comes not only with the process, but from the intent of the mother as well. Remember the Savior's words when he was in his own process of atoning? He said, "O Jerusalem, Jerusalem, [thou] that killest the prophets, and stonest them which are sent unto thee, how often would I have gathered thy children together, even as a hen gathereth her chickens under her wings, and ye would not" (Matthew 23:37).

Jesus spoke to the people of the Americas in the same manner:

4 O ye people of these great cities which have fallen, who are descendants of Jacob, yea, who are of the house of Israel, how oft have I gathered you as a hen gathereth her chickens under her wings, and have nourished you.

5 And again, how oft would I have gathered you as a hen gathereth her chickens under her wings, yea, O ye people of the house of Israel, who have fallen; yea, O ye people of the house of Israel, ye that dwell at Jerusalem, as ye that have fallen; yea, how oft would I have gathered you as a hen gathereth her chickens, and ye would not.

6 O ye house of Israel whom I have spared, how oft will I gather you as a hen gathereth her chickens under her wings, if ye will repent and return unto me with full purpose of heart. (3 Nephi 10:4–6)

Since the Restoration of the Gospel, the Savior's message and concern are the same. In the latter days, he has spoken, "For, behold, I will gather them as a hen gathereth her chickens under her wings, if they will not harden their hearts" (D&C 10:65).

He also declared, "Who will gather his people even as a hen gathereth her chickens under her wings, even as many as will hearken to my voice and humble themselves before me, and call upon me in mighty prayer" (D&C 29:2).

Furthermore, God proclaimed, "O, ye nations of the earth, how often would I have gathered you together as a hen gathereth her chickens under her wings, but ye would not" (D&C 43:24).

This process of a hen putting her chickens under her wing is a metaphor. It compares the act of a mother hen to the loving kindness of God. It is also the initiator of this next powerful message of being covered by the Atonement.

"tent of Israel" "stakes" and "wards"

The wonderful use of the idea of God covering all of his children is contained in the concept of a tent. Tents today are used for far different reasons than tents used by peoples who lived thousands of years ago. Therefore we might not attune ourselves to the message God intended by this symbol or idiom without some broadened effort. Today we use tents mostly for recreation as opposed to depending upon them for daily living. Our tents are made of modern materials and have ingenious ways to support themselves. When "pitching" a tent, we use procedures completely unknown to Abraham and Moses. Their tents were made of heavy hides of animals they had slain for their flesh for sustenance. They had not removed the hair from these hides, but they depended on the hair to insulate from the cold or heat and to shed the storms just as they had protected the animal from which they had been taken. These skins were stitched together and could be extended to increase the size and dimensions of the tent as time went on. How such a heavy tent would be pitched is the next consideration.

The first action would be to take a pole or "stake" and place it in the "center" area of the tent and then "raise" the stake upward so that the tent would begin to take the position of a covering. Next, the "borders" of the tent would be secured to the ground by pegs, or to rocks or trees, so that the center stake would not tip and fall. With that completed, other stakes or poles were added as additional support and to provide more covering under the tent. Such additions were made with stakes and hides until the tent was of sufficient size to cover all who want to be under its covering and protection.

Today, many members of the Church cannot explain the use of the words *stakes* and *wards*. They are words not chosen by Joseph Smith, but by the Lord. However, with the idea of the tent, the purpose and identity of "stakes" should become evident. Do not be confused by some who want to identify stakes as pegs or other devices used to secure the tent into position on the outer edge of the tent, but notice the use of this imagery by the Lord relative to the protection stakes will give: "Verily I say unto you all: Arise and shine forth, that thy light may be a standard for the nations; And that the gathering together upon the land of Zion, and upon her stakes, may be for a defense, and for a refuge from the storm, and from wrath when it shall be poured out without mixture upon the whole earth" (D&C 115:5–6).

This protection is the same as that spoken of by Isaiah regarding the latter-day glory of Israel. He wrote: "Enlarge the place of thy tent, and let them stretch forth the curtains of thine habitations: spare not, lengthen thy cords, and strengthen thy stakes" (Isaiah 54:2).

Regarding the millennial Zion, Isaiah exulted: "Look upon Zion, the city of our solemnities: thine eyes shall see Jerusalem a quiet habitation, a tabernacle that shall not be taken down; not one of the stakes thereof shall ever be removed, neither shall any of the cords thereof be broken" (Isaiah 33:20). The imagery of a tent, held up by stakes is clear.

Cords are needed to secure the tent. Isaiah saw a time when none of the stakes of the tent would be removed, nor would any of the supports be broken that hold up the covering of God's people—Zion.

"center stake of Zion"

In 1831, Joseph Smith designated where the center stake of Zion was. He said it was in Jackson County, Missouri (see D&C 57:3). However, a stake was not organized there. The first stake was organized in 1834, in Kirtland, Ohio. That seems to be a problem unless one looks at the figurative idea of the protection and the gathering of the saints under a covering of the Lord. The center stake does not have to be the very center of the tent! It is an idiom which indicates the beginning of the raising or pitching of the tent. The doctrines and ideas revealed relative to Jackson County, gave movement toward what happened in Kirtland and every stake organized or raised to support the tent of Zion since that time. The tent of Zion now is supported by thousands of stakes and its borders have been enlarged to provide spiritual shelter for millions throughout the world. It does not matter that the Kirtland stake was dissolved, and Salt Lake became the first stake organized that has continued until this day. The idea of import is the tent. The raising of the center stake was the indicator that the tent was being raised!

Some have spoken and taught that Jackson County, Missouri was called the "center stake" because geographically, Missouri is somewhat the center of the United States of America. But now that Zion has expanded far beyond the boundaries of North America, Jackson County, Missouri, is hardly the geographical center of Zion. Besides, a stake was not organized there until late in the twentieth century. The figurative idiom "center stake of Zion" is not literal. It is a metaphor.

Suppose you were watching Abraham's herdsmen raising their tent thousands of years ago, and you were describing what was taking place to someone unacquainted with the process. He might not be able to relate raising a tent to the preliminary work of unrolling the tent made of skins, positioning its door opening, and securing some of the borders of the patchwork of skins to the ground, rocks, or trees, to what was really happening. But when the herdsmen took a stake under the skins and began to raise the covering, the person you were with would exclaim, "Now I can see!"

And then you'd say, "That's just the center stake, wait till they add more stakes, then you really will see something grand!"

Much preparation work was done for the cause of Zion prior to the Jackson County experiences. But the Lord called what was done at the time the "center stake" for good reason. It could be compared to having someone at a ball game with you in a large stadium. You would see the players on the field doing all sorts of activities. Your friend might say to you, "When is it going to start?" You reply, "Just watch the flag pole down there. When the flag is raised to the top and the anthem song is finished, they will start the game."

Now the tent has been raised, enlarged, and strengthened, with new stakes added weekly. But imagine the heavenly cheers that ascended from hosts yet unborn, as well as those long gone from mortal life, when the "center stake" was erected, signaling that the tent or covering was standing, never to be removed!

What about wards? Considering the tender mercies of the Lord and his great concern for the care of us, his children, he has provided the protection of a covering, but he goes beyond that. He puts each of us into a ward. One of Webster's definitions for the word *ward* reads: "a person or body of persons under the protection or tutelage of a government."[3] The idea is stunning! We each are covered, but additionally, every member of the Church is in a ward and thereby under the protection and tutelage of God's government. That changes this common meaningless term from one of geographic dimensions to one that is reassuring because it infers that God is caring for and teaching us.

What if we are not under the Lord's tent? Then we should consider the words of Nephi as he quotes from Isaiah. He writes:

> 1 But, behold, in the last days, or in the days of the Gentiles—yea, behold all the nations of the Gentiles and also the Jews, both those who shall come upon this land and those who shall be upon other lands, yea, even upon all the lands of the earth, behold, they will be drunken with iniquity and all manner of abominations—
>
> 2 And when that day shall come they shall be visited of the Lord of Hosts, with thunder and with earthquake, and with a great noise, and with storm, and with tempest, and with the flame of devouring fire.
>
> 3 And all the nations that fight against Zion, and that distress her, shall be as a dream of a night vision; yea, it shall be unto them, even as unto a hungry man which dreameth, and behold he eateth but he awaketh and his soul is empty; or like unto a thirsty man which dreameth,

and behold he drinketh but he awaketh and behold he is faint, and his soul hath appetite; yea, even so shall the multitude of all the nations be that fight against Mount Zion. (2 Nephi 27:1–3).

The verses that follow make the reader so appreciative of having a place of refuge from such figurative conditions. But what kind of protection will the Lord give? Now, here comes the tutelage and knowledge that will save us from the storm! Starting in verse six, Nephi speaks words we should have high on our list of assurances. He writes:

> 6 And it shall come to pass that the Lord God shall bring forth unto you the words of a book, and they shall be the words of them which have slumbered.
>
> 7 And behold the book shall be sealed; and in the book shall be a revelation from God, from the beginning of the world to the ending thereof. (2 Nephi 27:6–7)

Nephi tells the wonderful things that will happen regarding this book as well as the truths it will teach. This is the way God protects. Read for yourself the rest of Nephi's promises. They are too many to include here. They go clear through the next three chapters. But remember, this entire discourse by Nephi follows his pinpointing the storms, tempests, thunder, noise, and devouring fire that will surround those under the tent of the Lord and not touch them. To be under God's tent is the only place where there will be safety in those days!

"Rock of Ages, cleft for me"

Great feelings generally result from singing or hearing the wonderful strains of the magnificent hymn "Rock of Ages." The words come so beautifully and with such power, but sometimes we don't consider the reasons why Augustus Montague Toplady chose the words he included in the hymn. His reference to the "Rock of Ages" is certainly Christ. Christ is symbolized as a rock because of his strength and stability. He is the same God who created the worlds and was with his father in the beginning (see Hebrews 1:1-3). Therefore, he is "The Rock of ages." But then the hymn continues, "Rock of Ages, cleft for me." What does that mean? What is a cleft? An unsubstantiated story says the lyrics were inspired when Toplady took shelter from a storm under a rocky overhang. An overhang or a cleft, which was to him a covering and hiding place from the storm. Covered! That is the whole message and essence of the Atonement, and Toplady wrote his hymn to give that message. The Savior is the rock and he provides an overhang, a cleft, a split, or a chasm in which he can hide or cover me.

1st verse:
Rock of Ages, cleft for me, Let me hide myself in thee;
Let the water and the blood, From thy wounded side which flowed,
Be of sin the double cure, Save from wrath and make me pure

3rd verse:
While I draw this fleeting breath, When mine eyes shall close in death,
When I rise to worlds unknown And behold thee on thy throne,
Rock of Ages, cleft for me, Let me hide myself in thee.

"bleed at every pore" "eat my flesh and drink my blood"

This phrase appears in the words of Christ as he answers questions regarding "endless torment" and "endless punishment." His definition determines for us that these terms should not be treated literally. We will not be subjected to torment or punishment endlessly, but we will be subjected to torment and punishment which are endless. There is a difference! If we do not repent on our own, then we will be punished, but we will be redeemed from that punishment. The Savior stated:

> 15 Therefore I command you to repent—repent, lest I smite you by the rod of my mouth, and by my wrath, and by my anger, and your sufferings be sore—how sore you know not, how exquisite you know not, yea, how hard to bear you know not.
>
> 16 For behold, I, God, have suffered these things for all, that they might not suffer if they would repent;
>
> 17 But if they would not repent they must suffer even as I;
>
> 18 Which suffering caused myself, even God, the greatest of all, to tremble because of pain, and to bleed at every pore, and to suffer both body and spirit—and would that I might not drink the bitter cup, and shrink—
>
> 19 Nevertheless, glory be to the Father, and I partook and finished my preparations unto the children of men. (D&C 19:15–19)

Did the Savior literally bleed from every pore? All the language within the surrounding verses is figurative. Consider the phrases such as "smite you by the rod of my mouth," (v. 15), "that I might not drink the bitter cup and shrink," (v. 18), "have tasted at the time I withdrew my Spirit," (v. 20); and "walk in the meekness of my Spirit" (v. 23). These phrases are figurative, not literal.

Amidst so many figurative expressions, what reason is there to consider "bleed from every pore," to be literal and be the only phrase that is? They are all idioms! They express more than the literal ever can express. Literal words are limited. Lovers even say, "I love you more than words can ever say."

Remember that the Savior taught figuratively so many times. To the Jews he testified that he was the one who gave their fathers "bread" or manna in the wilderness. Now he is the "bread" that his father had sent to them and they needed to, **"eat my flesh and drink my blood"** (John 6:53; emphasis added). What he taught in this metaphor is the same kind of message he taught when he said, "bleed at every pore." Remember that most of those who listened to him found it difficult to understand what he spoke since they had not been properly taught the teachings given to their fathers. They expected a messiah that would deliver them from their physical enemies and heal them of their physical infirmities. Little wonder they missed his symbolic or figurative teachings when he said:

> 49 Your fathers did eat manna in the wilderness, and are dead.
>
> 50 This is the bread which cometh down from heaven, that a man may eat thereof, and not die.
>
> 51 I am the living bread which came down from heaven: if any man eat of this bread, he shall live for ever: and the bread that I will give is my flesh, which I will give for the life of the world.
>
> 52 The Jews therefore strove among themselves, saying, How can this man give us his flesh to eat?
>
> 53 Then Jesus said unto them, Verily, verily, I say unto you, Except ye **eat the flesh** of the Son of man, and drink his blood, ye have no life in you. (John 6:49–53; emphasis added)

This idea of eating his flesh and drinking his blood is easily associated with partaking of the sacramental emblems. However, it is an idiom first, and teaches our need to take him entirely into our life. It isn't enough just to look at food, nor is it enough to taste a nibble of food set before us. We must consume it! And if we do, it will become a part of us. It is similar to one saying today that he "lives on sports." "He eats, sleeps and drinks baseball." For us today to think the same kinds of thoughts as we partake of the sacrament is very appropriate.

Many have spoken of the Savior's bleeding from every pore as an indicator of how intense his suffering was. Sometimes illustrations are given wherein, under certain perilous circumstances, one might bleed a small drop of blood. However, if one has this as the idea of what the Savior is saying, then one is interpreting this phenomenon as literal and missing the deep meaning intended. If a parent or loved one tells that they have gone through "blood, sweat, and tears," or "worked their fingers to the bone," what are they trying to really say? Their message is far beyond the literal.

When we use hyperbole, we try to illustrate something beyond the actual. That doesn't minimize the action or feeling, but conversely, it puts it in the realm of having no limits and going beyond even imagination. "I'm so hungry that I could eat an elephant" is such an idiomatic hyperbole. When using such a statement, we are attempting to take our thinking beyond anything possible. Another hyperbole is, "My heart bleeds for you." Neither of these idioms is possible but the person means that his concern or work is beyond anything that is plausible. Such is the idea of the Savior saying that he "bled from every pore." What he did was impossible for any mortal under any condition. For as Amulek taught:

> 9 For it is expedient that an atonement should be made; for according to the great plan of the Eternal God there must be an atonement made, or else all mankind must unavoidably perish; yea, all are hardened; yea, all are fallen and are lost, and must perish except it be through the Atonement which it is expedient should be made.
>
> 10 For it is expedient that there should be a great and last sacrifice; yea, not a sacrifice of man, neither of beast, neither of any manner of fowl; for it shall not be a human sacrifice; but it must be an infinite and eternal sacrifice.
>
> 11 Now there is not any man that can sacrifice his own blood which will atone for the sins of another. (Alma 34:9–11)

What was Amulek's message? It was that the sacrifice that was made was not mortal! Bleeding from every pore is mortal. But Christ's suffering was beyond mortal.

When Luke makes his statement of the agony of the Savior in

Gethsemane, he uses the comparative "as it were." His account reads, "And being in an agony he prayed more earnestly: and his sweat was as it were great drops of blood falling down to the ground" (Luke 22:44).

Alma uses similar words to describe the great efforts of his armies in defending the people who should have provided necessities to sustain them in their military struggles with their enemies. He wrote: "But behold, this is not all—ye have withheld your provisions from them, insomuch that many have fought and **bled out their lives** because of their great desires which they had for the welfare of this people; yea, and this they have done when they were about to perish with hunger, because of your exceedingly great neglect towards them" (Alma 60:9; emphasis added).

His army survived even though they had "bled out their lives." Idioms tell of feelings and efforts far better than literal statements. Literal statements only tell what is possible and understandable. Therefore, the things they describe are things and emotions that can be replicated and are within limits. However, figurative language takes us beyond the describable and only is limited by parameters such as infinite and eternal. These are the descriptions of the Savior's Atonement. If his suffering was of actual drops of blood, then someone else could do the same.

The Savior's actual dying precipitates the same kinds of questions. He was subjected to scourging, piercing, whipping, beating, thirsting, and humiliation. However, if this is the focus of our attention, then we have to conclude that the Savior's death was the worst physical death ever suffered by anyone who ever lived. Physically that is not the case. Many artists have depicted the thieves crucified on either side of the Savior. Clearly, the thieves are only tied and not nailed to their crosses. If you ask why the artists portray their crucifixion in this manner, the reason generally will be to make the Savior's suffering worse than theirs.

The Savior's physical suffering was not the whole sum of his suffering and his love for us. If so, someone else could possibly claim to have suffered a worse punishment and death. But Christ's suffering indicates that he was God's Son, who had the power to lay down his life and the power to take it up again. He thus had the power to save all mankind from their death and their sins. The most terrible element is that he was rejected and abused. He was himself a God, and the Creator of all. He gave his life so that he could break the bands of death and give all the Resurrection. He was also the only one who knew of our sins, past, present, and future. He alone perfectly knew of our father's plan of redemption and love for us. That is what made his ordeal unique. No one else could ever endure that! No one else had that power. His own Resurrection would make it possible for us to be resurrected and thus put us in position to be heirs to kingdoms of glory. No one else could do that! His physical suffering was terrible. However, that is from a mortal point of view.

No child knows the love and lengths a parent will go through for him. So it is that understanding what Christ did is beyond us as mortals. It was much more than the whips, nails, thorns, and cross. These are only indicators and symbols of what he did. Symbols can never be more significant than the principles which they represent.

Many individuals of great faith have commented regarding these words "bled from every pore" using a literal interpretation. However, it is hoped that consideration can be given to the idiomatic design used by our Redeemer as he described his atoning work in a revelation to Martin Harris in his own words. Section 19 of the Doctrine and Covenants is spoken in first person by the Savior himself.

"washed in the blood of the Lamb" "washed in his blood" "cleansed by the blood of Christ"

Here is an idiom that is beyond practical thinking for most of today's culture. Nothing in modern society corresponds to the idea of blood as a cleansing agent. Blood on a fabric is avoided and dreaded more than any other stain. Physicians and dentists wear protection by masking themselves while performing even the simplest of procedures. Sports participants cannot continue to play if they have any blood on them or on their uniforms. We have been taught in recent years that blood, even a speck of it can transfer disease and infection. We fear such exposure. We are far removed in feelings regarding blood from our ancestors who had no fear of blood—human or animal. Blood was often considered a sign of the price of victory. However, blood is still associated with cleansing in past and present religious language.

To understand such rhetoric, we need to know that blood is the transportation system of the body for all infection, toxins, and waste. It not only supplies nutrients and oxygen to every living cell in our bodies, but it transports all deadly elements back to organs that remove the same from the blood before it is enriched and returned to resupply our bodies again. This is why the Lord commanded that blood was not to be consumed and that animals were to be bled out before the flesh of their bodies was eaten (see Genesis 9:4–5; Leviticus 3:17). Our bodies are cleansed by the blood. This is why we find such beautiful figurative expressions regarding the blood of Christ. It is because he will cleanse us, or our garments, from our sins the same as our own blood cleanses our bodies of things that would surely kill us.

Jesus spoke of his father's kingdom in these words to the Nephites: "And no unclean thing can enter into his kingdom; therefore nothing entereth into his rest save it be those who have washed their garments in my blood, because of their faith, and the repentance of all their sins, and their faithfulness unto the end" (3 Nephi 27:19).

Alma taught his people: "I say unto you, ye will know at that day that ye cannot be saved; for there can no man be saved except his garments are washed white; yea, his garments must be purified until they are cleansed from all stain, through the blood of him of whom it has been spoken by our fathers, who should come to redeem his people from their sins" (Alma 5:21).

John the Revelator wrote of those who would be inheritors of dominions. They would wear robes which would identify them as rulers. "And I said unto him, Sir, thou knowest. And he said to me, These are they which came out of great tribulation, and have washed their robes, and made them white in the blood of the Lamb" (Revelation 7:14).

John began his revelation with an introduction and greeting from Jesus. He wrote: "And from Jesus Christ, who is the faithful witness, and the first begotten of the dead, and the prince of the kings of the earth. Unto him that loved us, and washed us from our sins in his own blood" (Revelation 1:5).

John wrote the same message in his first general epistle to the Church. He admonished, "But if we walk in the light, as he is in the light, we have fellowship one with another, and the blood of Jesus Christ his Son cleanseth us from all sin" (1 John 1:7).

Powerful and beautiful references telling of cleansing by the blood of Christ are found thoughout the scriptures. Only a few are cited here. However, the figurative use of the blood of Christ does not end just with his blood. We next examine another idiom.

"body of Christ"

The expression "body of Christ" is also abundantly used in scriptural writing. However, reading the surrounding words to the idiom is the only way to determine if it references those believers who follow Christ and are considered a body of believers, or if the idiom relates to Christ's own blood and body figuratively. If the figurative message of his blood cleansing us is in effect, then figuratively we have need to be part of his body in order for his blood to flow through us and cleanse us. Notice the words of the Apostle Paul to the Corinthians, slightly changed by Joseph Smith, "Flee fornication. Every sin that a man committeth is against the body of Christ, and he who committeth fornication sinneth against his own body" (JST 1 Corinthians 6:18).

Figurative expressions often have more than one application or similitude. When this is the case, it is called dualism. With this in mind, perhaps every inference to the "body of Christ" should be considered as suggesting that we are figuratively part of his body so that his blood, figuratively, can go through us and cleanse us. If we are called the body of Christ only because we believe and are part of the body or group of those that do believe in him, perhaps we are missing the dualistic message regarding his blood and body. To apply the significance of this idiom expands it and gives it a wonderful new association. It also gives additional significance to referring to the Savior as the "great physician." The Savior himself brought forth the challenge on the day he read from the writings of Isaiah in the synagogue in Nazareth, and declared himself to be the promised Messiah of whom Isaiah prophesied. "And he said unto them, Ye will surely say unto me this proverb, Physician, heal thyself: whatsoever we have heard done in Capernaum, do also here in thy country" (Luke 4:23).

The people who heard Jesus were only concerned about his power to heal them of their physical infirmities as he had done in other cities. The Savior's healing of the physically infirm was primarily testimony that if he had the power to heal them physically, then he could heal their souls from sin and death. It was affirmation that his blood could heal and cleanse them from all sin.

"blotted out"

We have great promises from God that our sins will be "blotted out." "Have mercy upon me, O God, according to thy lovingkindness: according unto the multitude of thy tender mercies **blot out my transgressions**" (Psalms 51:1; emphasis added).

We all are beyond the times when blotters were used to absorb excess ink from quills and pens. We may have forgotten the difference between blotting and erasing. Our sins are not going to simply be erased or "whited out." They are going to be "taken on" by the Savior. Peter proclaimed, "Repent ye therefore, and be converted, that your sins may be blotted out, when the times of refreshing shall come from the presence of the Lord" (Acts 3:19).

Alma taught, "Now the Spirit knoweth all things; nevertheless the Son of God suffereth according to the flesh that he might **take upon him the sins** of his people, that **he might blot out** their transgressions according to the power of his deliverance; and now behold, this is the testimony which is in me" (Alma 7:13; emphasis added).

Amulek testified in the same manner, "And now, behold, I will testify unto you of myself that these things are true. Behold, I say unto you, that I do know that Christ shall come among the children of men, to **take upon him** the transgressions of his people, and that he shall atone for the sins of the world; for the Lord God hath spoken it" (Alma 34:8; emphasis added).

The caring, saving approach of our Savior to take upon himself our sins is overwhelming in its significance and devotion. For us to think that our sins are just erased and vanish away with no affect is not correct doctrine. The word *blot* carries that message of our Savior absorbing the sins of all who will hear and believe. Other references which contain the words "blotted out" speak of the unrepentant having their "names blotted out." The idea of erasing may be more appropriate for these instances; however, the idiom may well be applied that we never are erased, but taken on by the Savior (Revelation 3:5; Mosiah 26:36; D&C 20:83).

Notes

1. Russell M. Nelson, "The Atonement," *Ensign*, Nov. 1996, 34.
2. Joseph F. McConkie, *Gospel Symbolism* (Salt Lake City: Bookcraft, 1985), 138.
3. *Merriam-Webster's Collegiate Dictionary* (Merriam-Webster: Springfield, MA, 2003), "ward."
4. "Rock of Ages," *Hymns* no. 111.

IDIOMS REGARDING OUR RELATIONSHIP WITH GOD

"broken heart"

These two words may seem to be only a simple statement of contrition. However, the word *broken*, like so many words in English, has other definitions. To understand another interpretation of the word *broken* we must consider the word *testament*. In both Hebrew and Aramaic, as well as in Greek, the word for *testament* is the very same word for *covenant*. In Greek the word is *diatheke*. That is why the New Testament is so named—because it is the record of the New Covenant that now applies in the plan of salvation. Under the Old Covenant, or the Old Testament, the promise of Heavenly Father was for all to repent of their sins and he would send a savior to redeem them from the result of those sins. When the Savior did come, the message changed to one that said to repent because God had given his son as a sacrifice for the sins we had committed. The new covenant also covered all those who would commit sin in the future and all of us yet unborn when the new covenant was put into effect. That is the reason for the name change for the Book of Mormon in 1986. The name was changed from "The Book of Mormon" to "The Book of Mormon, Another Testament of Jesus Christ." The Lord himself was the originator for this idea. In speaking of the Book of Mormon and its use after its publication, the Lord said, "And they shall remain under this condemnation until they repent and remember the **new covenant**, even the Book of Mormon and the former commandments which I have given them, not only to say, but to do according to that which I have written" (D&C 84:57; emphasis added).[1]

The exchanging or substituting to the word *covenant* and *testament* is observed in the new title of the book. So it is important to understand these two words and the messages they transmit. However, we must go back to the word *diatheke* and look for the full range of its meaning. It also suggests cutting or breaking in addition to making a covenant and giving a testimony of such. Cutting is often associated, in our English speaking, with covenant making when people say such things as, "I will cut you a good deal." Breaking has also been long associated with covenant making by inviting someone to "break bread" with you. Breaking bread may include actual bread at a meal; however, its significance goes far beyond that single action. It suggests that you would make covenants or renew the binding relationships into which you already had entered. That is the whole idea of Jesus breaking bread and giving it to each of his apostles. It was an event designed to make new covenants and strengthen the covenants they had already made. It was *diatheke*.

Little wonder that when we, on the Sabbath day, are expected to think of covenants when we see the priesthood holders break the bread in front of the congregation. They are not just making enough pieces so that each person may have some bread. They are declaring, as with the shrill blasts of trumpets or shofar, to "watch us break the bread, for here is your opportunity to covenant with your God."

Now we can and should associate this word *break*, with this new but yet old meaning, in the idiom "broken heart." In scriptural settings, it should suggest "covenant heart" or "covenant hearted." Notice the message in the following verses if you apply this definition.

- And ye shall offer for a sacrifice unto me a broken heart and a contrite spirit. And whoso cometh unto me with a **broken heart** and a contrite spirit, him will I baptize with fire and with the Holy Ghost, even as the Lamanites, because of their faith in me at the time of their conversion, were baptized with fire and with the Holy Ghost, and they knew it not. (3 Nephi 9:20; emphasis added)

- And behold, I have given you the law and the commandments of my Father, that ye shall believe in me, and that ye shall repent of your sins, and come unto me with a **broken heart** and a contrite spirit. Behold, ye have the commandments before you, and the law is fulfilled. (3 Nephi 12:19; emphasis added)
- Behold, when ye shall rend that veil of unbelief which doth cause you to remain in your awful state of wickedness, and hardness of heart, and blindness of mind, then shall the great and marvelous things which have been hid up from the foundation of the world from you—yea, when ye shall call upon the Father in my name, with a **broken heart** and a contrite spirit, then shall ye know that the Father hath remembered the covenant which he made unto your fathers, O house of Israel. (Ether 4:15; emphasis added)
- Neither did they receive any unto baptism save they came forth with a **broken heart** and a contrite spirit, and witnessed unto the church that they truly repented of all their sins. (Moroni 6:2; emphasis added)
- But blessed are the poor who are pure in heart, whose **hearts are broken**, and whose spirits are contrite, for they shall see the kingdom of God coming in power and great glory unto their deliverance; for the fatness of the earth shall be theirs. (D&C 56:18; emphasis added)
- Thou shalt offer a sacrifice unto the Lord thy God in righteousness, even that of a **broken heart** and a contrite spirit. (D&C 59:8; emphasis added)
- The Lord is nigh unto them that are of a **broken heart**; and saveth such as be of a contrite spirit. (Psalms 34:18; emphasis added)

In verse and in song, we often sing of the Savior being "bruised, broken, torn for us."[2] Yes, he was beaten, and blood came from his wounds, but is that the only or full intent of such words? Saying that he had kept the covenant he had made with our Father in Heaven, as well as with us, comes strongly through the words *broken* and *torn*. What a beautiful message! It is far different from the idea that generally comes from gazing upon our Lord's grief-stricken face and hopeless expression that is displayed in many religious art forms. It changes that grief and hopelessness to the message of accomplishment and victory. Truly, "broken heart" is an idiom. It tells far more when we look beyond the literal. The Savior did die because of a broken heart—a covenant heart.

"worthy to stand"

The idea of standing before God is the opposite of "upon thy belly thou shalt go" as found in the dialogue in the Garden of Eden. As we learned previously, there it is written: "And the Lord God said unto the serpent, Because thou hast done this, thou art cursed above all cattle, and above every beast of the field; upon thy belly shalt thou go, and dust shalt thou eat all the days of thy life" (Genesis 3:14). Being upon one's belly, as opposed to standing, appears in modern expressions such as, "She kicked him out of the house, but he came crawling back the next morning. He had to lick her boots before she would let him back in."

"Eating dust" indicates that you will not lead or be out in front to lead. Eating dust is following the caravan or herd. Today one might say, "My car is lots faster than yours. Let's race and I'll make you eat dust."

Regarding having the ability to stand, the Lord has said, "Watch ye therefore, and pray always, that ye may be accounted worthy to escape all these things that shall come to pass, and **to stand** before the Son of man" (Luke 21:36). In the latter days God has said:

- "He that is slothful shall not be counted **worthy to stand**, and he that learns not his duty and shows himself not approved shall not be counted worthy to stand. Even so. Amen" (D&C 107:100).
- "Behold, the great day of the Lord is at hand; and who can abide the day of his coming, and who **can stand** when he appeareth?" (D&C 128:24).

Being "worthy to stand" is figurative just like "upon thy belly shalt thou go." Both of their messages are far beyond the literal meaning of the words.

"shall see me" "has seen God"

Because of the limitations of our English language, the word *see* can portray multiple meanings. Many English words do the same.

Some illustrations of this are *light, picture, head*, and *rock*. One usage will be a verb while another can be a noun or adverb. In a revelation received by Joseph Smith in 1831, we can observe multiple uses of the word *see*. The reason for the revelation was to reaffirm that the revelations in the soon to be published Book of Commandments were from God. The Lord assured:

> 10 And again, verily I say unto you that it is your privilege, and a promise I give unto you that have been ordained unto this ministry, that inasmuch as you strip yourselves from jealousies and fears, and humble yourselves before me, for ye are not sufficiently humble, the veil shall be rent and **you shall see me** and know that I am—not with the carnal neither natural **mind**, but with the spiritual.
>
> 11 For no man **has seen God** at any time in the flesh, except quickened by the Spirit of God.
>
> 12 Neither can any natural man abide the presence of God, neither after the carnal mind.
>
> 13 Ye are not able to abide the presence of God now, neither the ministering of angels; wherefore, continue in patience until ye are perfected.
>
> 14 Let not your minds turn back; and when ye are worthy, in mine own due time, **ye shall see** and know that which was conferred upon you by the hands of my servant Joseph Smith, Jun. Amen" (D&C 67:10–14; emphasis added)

Note that the Lord stated that they would be able to see him, not with the carnal neither natural mind, but with the spiritual. He did not say they would see him with the eye, but with the mind. He further seems to associate abiding in his presence with seeing him, neither of which could occur with a carnal mind unless they were quickened by the Spirit. Then in verse 14 he uses the word *see* as having nothing to do with the eye, but an understanding of the heart or mind.

In the great revelation identified by Joseph Smith as "the olive leaf," there are numerous idioms. Starting in verse 63, there are at least a dozen phrases whose connotation is not literal and, thereby, whose limits are boundless. "Shall see him" is among all these idioms and there are no indicators that it should be considered atypical from all the rest. Consider the idioms highlighted in the verses:

> 63 **Draw near unto me** and **I will draw near unto you**; **seek me diligently** and **ye shall find me**; **ask, and ye shall receive**; **knock,**

and it shall be opened unto you.

64 Whatsoever ye ask the Father in my name it shall be given unto you, that is expedient for you;

65 And if ye ask anything that is not expedient for you, it shall turn unto your condemnation.

66 Behold, that which **you hear** is as **the voice** of one **crying in the wilderness**—in the wilderness, **because you cannot see him**—my voice, **because my voice is Spirit**; **my Spirit is truth**; truth abideth and hath no end; and **if it be in you it shall abound**.

67 And if your eye be single to my glory, your whole bodies shall be filled with light, and there shall be no darkness in you; and that body which is filled with light comprehendeth all things.

68 Therefore, sanctify yourselves that your minds **become single to God**, and the days will come that **you shall see him**; for he will **unveil his face** unto you, and it shall be **in his own time**, and **in his own way**, and according to his own will. (D&C 88:63–68; emphasis added)

In verses prior to those just noted, similar verses illustrate the Lord describing things that only some would understand. They are not straightforward to many, and their meaning is determined by the understanding of the hearer. The Lord declares:

46 Unto what shall I liken these kingdoms, that ye may understand?

47 Behold, all these are kingdoms, and any man who hath seen any or the least of these hath seen God moving in his majesty and power.

48 I say unto you, he hath seen him; nevertheless, he who came unto his own was not comprehended.

49 The light shineth in darkness, and the darkness comprehendeth it not; nevertheless, the day shall come when you shall comprehend even God, being quickened in him and by him.

50 Then shall ye know that **ye have seen me**, that I am, and that I am the true light that is in you, and that you are in me; otherwise ye could not abound. (D&C 88:46–50; emphasis added)

Isn't it interesting that the Lord doesn't just say "ye have seen me?" Rather, he states, "Then shall ye know that ye have seen me." Evidently, it isn't enough just to see, but we must also know.

The idiom "face to face" means that two people speaking face to face do not need a mediator. Two individuals could stand before each other, look at one another, and yet not see "eye to eye" or "face to face. Conversely, two individuals can speak over the telephone and though they can never see one another physically, they can say that they see "eye to eye" and "face to face." The idiom tells of how they feel much more than a physical experience. We might hear someone say, "I know what he said to you, but I've just got to talk to him face to face." Why? Because the face displays much emotion. Every wrinkle and squint, every glimmer, grimace, and facial twitch, tells far more than what the voice says. That is the constant challenge—to be in harmony with God and his will. There is no better way to say it than "see him 'face to face.' " This idiom "face to face" is used more than twenty times in scripture. It suggests being open, being understood plainly, and hiding nothing. Therefore, there is no need for a mediator or arbitrator. We speak as friends (Exodus 33:11).

In the *Improvement Era*, of 1966, the following was published as the message of the First Presidency and the Council of the Twelve:

> The question frequently arises: "Is it necessary for a member of the Council of the Twelve to see the Savior in order to be an apostle?" Answer: It is their privilege to see Him if occasion requires, but the Lord has taught that there is a stronger witness than seeing a personage, even of seeing the Son of God in a vision. Impressions on the soul that come from the Holy Ghost are far more significant than a vision. When Spirit speaks to spirit, the imprint upon the soul is far more difficult to erase. Every member of the Church should have impressions that Jesus is the Son of God indelibly pictured on his soul through the witness of the Holy Ghost.[3]

"know thee"

The word *know* is another common word with multiple meanings. It can mean that we have met someone, and therefore know him. It can be a sexual euphemism, indicating intercourse. It can indicate having knowledge about someone or something. This could cause one to say, "I know him. I know what he will do." Jesus prayed to God, the Father, "And this is life eternal, that they might know thee the only true God, and Jesus Christ, whom thou hast sent" (John 17:3). Our goal should be to know the mind of God, and also to know the will of God. We must also strive to know that our life is pleasing to God. It is not enough just to know the "story." We must know him. These truths will only be made manifest to us through the Holy Spirit.

"arm of the Lord" "in the arms of Jesus" "open arms" "arms of my love" "arms of mercy"

Because different parts of the body are unique both in shape and function, they make excellent symbols. Parts of the body are also used as symbols because everyone knows can relate to body parts and their functions. The arm is considered a symbol of power.

Note the use of this idea in the following verses:

- And then cometh the day when the **arm** of the Lord shall be revealed in **power** in convincing the nations, the heathen nations, the house of Joseph, of the gospel of their salvation (D&C 90:10; emphasis added).

- And the **arm of the Lord** shall be revealed; and the day cometh that they who will not hear the voice of the Lord, neither the voice of his servants, neither give heed to the words of the prophets and apostles, shall be cut off from among the people (D&C 1:14; emphasis added).

- Yea, even doth not Isaiah say: Who hath believed our report, and to whom is the **arm of the Lord** revealed? (Mosiah 14:1; emphasis added).

- That the saying of Esaias the prophet might be fulfilled, which he spake, Lord, who hath believed our report? and to whom hath the **arm of the Lord been revealed**? (John 12:38, emphasis added).

- Who hath believed our report? and to whom is the **arm of the Lord revealed**? (Isaiah 53:1; emphasis added)

Mormon lamented over the destruction of his people and spoke the following words as his wish:

- For I know that such will sorrow for the calamity of the house of Israel; yea, they will sorrow for the destruction of this people; they will sorrow that this people had not repented that they might have been clasped in the **arms of Jesus** (Mormon 5:11; emphasis added).

- O ye fair ones, how could ye have departed from the ways of the Lord! O ye fair ones, how could ye have rejected that Jesus, who stood with **open arms** to receive you! (Mormon 6:17; emphasis added).

These idiomatic expressions suggest the love of God, but the idea of his omnipotent power should be considered first as being suggested by the idiom. The same is true for the idiom "**the arms of my love.**" The Lord said to Oliver Cowdery, "Behold, thou art Oliver, and I have spoken unto thee because of thy desires; therefore treasure up these words in thy heart. Be faithful and diligent in keeping the commandments of God, and I will encircle thee in the **arms of my love**" (D&C 6:20; emphasis added).

Having the Savior literally take us each into his arms is not the message of these idioms. As wondrous as such a literal experience would be, it would not include the guarantee of forgiveness of sin or that we had complied with God's commands. A literal interpretation would only suggest a compassionate act, an act that might be expected for each and every sinner. But the idea of this figurative message is that if we are in the arms of the Savior's love, we have been redeemed. That transcends all other ideas of understanding and compassion. Nephi received a personal knowledge of his standing with the Lord. He doesn't speak of any certain literal experience; however, he uses this most sublime expression, "But behold, the Lord hath redeemed my soul from hell; I have beheld his glory, and I am encircled about eternally in the arms of his love" (2 Nephi 1:15).

Similar meaning comes out of the teachings of Mormon when he laments for the disobedient of the house of Israel. He wrote: "For I know that such will sorrow for the calamity of the house of Israel; yea, they will sorrow for the destruction of this people; they will sorrow that this people had not repented that they might have been **clasped in the arms of Jesus**" (Mormon 5:11; emphasis added).

Mormon also bemoaned: "O ye fair ones, how could ye have departed from the ways of the Lord! O ye fair ones, how could ye have rejected that Jesus, who stood **with open arms to receive you**! (Mormon 6:17; emphasis added).

Alma used the same expression of the power that God has as he spoke of the mercy that comes to those who repent. He said, "And thus mercy can satisfy the demands of justice, and **encircles them in the arms of safety**, while he that exercises no faith unto repentance is exposed to the whole law of the demands of justice; therefore only unto him that has faith unto repentance is brought about the great and eternal plan of redemption" (Alma 34:16; emphasis added). Previously he had said, "Behold, he sendeth an invitation unto all men, for the **arms of mercy** are extended towards them, and he saith: Repent, and I will receive you" (Alma 5:33; emphasis added).

Again, Alma emphasized that we can have God's arms or power surround us. Remember he said, "And thus mercy can satisfy the demands of justice, and **encircles them in the arms of safety**, while he that exercises no faith unto repentance is exposed to the whole law of the demands of justice; therefore only unto him that has faith unto repentance is brought about the great and eternal plan of redemption" (Alma 34:16; emphasis added).

The prophet Abinadi, while in chains, taught in King Noah's court that those who refused to repent would never achieve the power of mercy. He said, "Having gone according to their own carnal wills and desires; having never called upon the Lord while **the arms of mercy** were extended towards them; for **the arms of mercy** were extended towards them, and they would not; they being warned of their iniquities and yet they would not depart from them; and they were commanded to repent and yet they would not repent" (Mosiah 16:12; emphasis added).

"ye are my friends"

This statement made by Jesus to the Twelve seems like a straightforward declaration. However, by carefully reading the surrounding verses, one can see that it is an idiom. Jesus said, "Ye are my friends, **if** ye do whatsoever I command you" (John 15:14; emphasis added). That little word "if" differentiates between those whom Jesus calls friends and those who are servants. The next verse compares those whom he calls "servants" with those who are "friends." It reads, "Henceforth I call you not servants; for the *servant knoweth not* what his Lord doeth: but I have called you friends; for all things that I have heard of my Father *I have made known unto you*" (John 15:15; emphasis added).

By this definition, to be a friend to Jesus, we must do more than just spend time together and be companions. We must "know" him and know his needs so that we can do the things which he needs done, without him even telling us to do them. The Savior told his disciples that "all things that I have heard of my Father I have made known unto you." That makes it possible for them to be his friends if they will just act accordingly. Servants are not told the why's of their service. They only do what they are told.

If you say, "Jesus is my friend," but only because you feel a relationship with him, that may not be the definition inferred by the idiom. A possible test to see if we are friends with Jesus might be to ask some questions like, "Did I do my home or visiting teaching last month?" Even if the answer is in the affirmative, it is interesting to ask further, "Why did you do it?" If the answer is, "Because I don't want to be on the report for those who didn't complete the assignment," then that may be an indicator that we are friendly with Jesus, but may not be his "friend."

- Question: "Why are you going on your mission?"
- Answer: "Because I feel that this is what Jesus needs me to do." Wow! What an answer and what vision!
- Question: "Why are you making certain you are being married in the temple?"
- Answer: "Because this is what God wants me to do." These last two answers would be in contrast to possible answers of, "because all my friends are going," or "my parents want me to be married there."

In 1832, elders began returning in the month of September from missions in the eastern states. This was a season of joy, for so many were working at doing the will of the Lord without compulsion. To those priesthood holders, Jesus spoke, "And as I said unto mine apostles, even so I say unto you, for you are mine apostles, even God's high priests; ye are they whom my Father hath given me; **ye are my friends**" (D&C 84:63; emphasis added). Surely this has to be one of the most endearing things that we ever could hear said to us by the Lord—"Ye are my friend." It means far more than the words alone.

"the true vine" John 15:1

In the tenth "I Am" statement, recorded by John in his gospel, Jesus asserts that;

> 1 I am **the true vine**, and my Father is the husbandman.
>
> 2 Every branch in me that beareth not fruit he taketh away: and every branch that beareth fruit, he purgeth it, that it may bring forth more fruit.
>
> 3 Now ye are clean through the word which I have spoken unto you.

4 Abide in me, and I in you. As the branch cannot bear fruit of itself, except it abide in the vine; no more can ye, except ye abide in me.

5 I am the vine, ye are the branches: He that abideth in me, and I in him, the same bringeth forth much fruit: for without me ye can do nothing.

6 If a man abide not in me, he is cast forth as a branch, and is withered; and men gather them, and cast them into the fire, and they are burned.

7 If ye abide in me, and my words abide in you, ye shall ask what ye will, and it shall be done unto you.

8 Herein is my Father glorified, that ye bear much fruit; so shall ye be my disciples. (John 15:1–8; emphasis added)

This statement of being the true vine seems to come out of nowhere and be an independent teaching of the Savior. The chapter begins with his statement of being the true vine and has no preface such as "As Jesus neared the entrance of the temple, he noticed the vine there and said. . . ." However it is helpful to know that everyone in Israel understood his teaching regarding the vine and its branches. On the temple there was a "golden vine with grape clusters hanging from it, a marvel of size and artistry."[4] This vine was also used to represent Jerusalem on coins made during the first Jewish revolt (AD 66–70). It may well have its origin in "Yet I had planted thee a noble vine, wholly a right seed: how then art thou turned into the degenerate plant of a strange vine unto me?" (Jeremiah 2:21).

Prominent in Church architecture even today, these clusters of grapes are still noticeable in such buildings as the tabernacle in St. George, Utah, completed in 1874. The grapes represent the concept of Israel. Scriptural references in latter-day revelations regarding fruit, grapes, vineyards and being planted, likely have this same emphasis. Most notable among these is the parable contained in a revelation in 1831 regarding the beginnings of gathering in Missouri. It is told in D&C 101:43–64.

Jesus was surely making reference to this concept of Israel being likened to a vine. He declared that he was that vine and compared himself to the vine on the temple. He proclaimed that unlike the vine on the temple made out of stone with golden leaves and fruit, "I am the true vine" and "ye are the branches." The main point of the allegory is that there is a union between Jesus and his followers. The disciples' very lives depended upon this union. As branches, believers either bear fruit and are pruned to bear more fruit, or do not bear fruit and are pruned and thrown away to be burned (John 15:6).

"calves of the stall" 1 Nephi 22:24, Malachi 4:2

Nephi had been reading from the brass plates that told of the last days. His brothers asked him what the things he read meant. He spoke of the gathering of Israel from the isles of the sea where they had been hidden, and then spoke of a time when the righteous would not need to fear for the churches which had been built up to get gain would be brought low in the dust and be consumed as stubble. This gives us an idea of the time frame because of what follows that declaration. He announces, "And the time cometh speedily that the righteous must be led up as **calves of the stall**, and the Holy One of Israel must reign in dominion, and might, and power, and great glory" (1 Nephi 22:24; emphasis added). He is speaking of times just prior to the Millennium. This is also supported by the following verses that tell of the return of Elijah in 1836 and the restoration of the keys he holds.

Such an idiom adds great value to our life and should be understood. The opposite condition to a calf being raised in a stall would be for it to be raised in the open range. There it would graze on whatever it chose to eat and bed down in whatever place suited it, safe or not. It would be watered from sources it found itself. This is an allegorical teaching. Nephi said that there would be in the last days a time when the righteous would be led up as calves of the stall. Such an idiom means that the righteous would be fed what their master would like them to consume, be safely bedded or tended, and have safe water always before them.

As we approach the millennial era, the righteous should expect to be fed and cared for spiritually by the master and his servants. Allegorically, some calves will push against the restraints of the stall. They will wish unwisely for freedom in nutrition and action. And so it is. Many object today to being "brought up in the Church." However, wise saints should learn to enjoy the blessings of being calves of the stall and being nourished by the word of the Lord. We should not be outside the stall where there is danger and alternate choices.

Malachi used the same phrase in a verse that precedes the promise of Elijah's return to turn the heart of the fathers to the children and the heart of the children to the fathers.

"But unto you that fear my name shall the Sun of righteousness arise with healing in his wings; and ye shall go forth, and grow up as **calves of the stall**" (Malachi 4:2; emphasis added). What a wonderful idiom to describe the conditions for the righteous! Leaders are in control of that which we are fed from the pulpit and in the classroom. We are told to limit our exposure to the world even if the grass often looks greener on the other side of the fence.

Notes

1. For a full account of the name change of the Book of Mormon, see Ezra Taft Benson, "The Book of Mormon—Keystone of Our Religion," *Ensign*, Nov. 1986, 4.
2. "Jesus of Nazareth, Savior and King," *Hymns* no. 181, second verse.
3. Joseph Fielding Smith, "The First Presidency and the Council of the Twelve," *Improvement Era*, Nov. 1966, 979.
4. Josephus, *Antiquity of the Jews*, 15:395.

IDIOMS REGARDING THE NATURE AND CHARACTER OF GOD

"finger of God"

The fingers on our hand are used for doing many things. They are the workmen of the body. However, when the singular expression is used of just one finger, the message of communicating direction or singling out some element or action is conveyed by the pointing of the finger. A literal rendering of what the Lord gave or did upon Sinai, in regards to the tablets of stone that contained the Ten Commandments, would have the Lord's finger be as a pen or an engraver. The verse in question reads: "And he gave unto Moses, when he had made an end of communing with him upon mount Sinai, two tables of testimony, tables of stone, written with the finger of God" (Exodus 31:18). However, a literal rendition is not appropriate for what Jesus told those who doubted his divinity. He said, "But if I with the finger of God cast out devils, no doubt the kingdom of God is come upon you" (Luke 11:20). In both verses the idiom "finger of God" is telling that the action was under God's direction. If devils were cast out, it would not be under the direction of mortal man. Likewise, the commandments from Sinai were not given by Moses, but came under God's direction.

The same message is embraced in the record of Alma. He wrote of what Amulek spoke, "I am Amulek; I am the son of Giddonah, who was the son of Ishmael, who was a descendant of Aminadi; and it was the same Aminadi who interpreted the writing which was upon the wall of the temple, which was written by the finger of God." (Alma 10:2). It doesn't matter how or by whom it was written. The statement made is that what is being read is God's will. It is flawless. It was given under God's direction. Among many other uses of this idiom are these examples: Moses 6:46; Exodus 8:19; and Deuteronomy 9:10.

"hand of the Lord" "hand of God" "God's handiwork" "the Lord's hand is not shortened"

The hand is the implement of action. It does work, gives comfort and reassurance, and protects and provides. That is the message regarding the work of the disciples recorded by Luke. He wrote, "And the hand of the Lord was with them: and a great number believed, and turned unto the Lord" (Acts 11:21).

Nephi wrote concerning the land which had been given to his father's seed, the American continent, "Wherefore, I, Lehi, prophesy according to the workings of the Spirit which is in me, that there shall none come into this land save they shall be brought by the **hand of the Lord**" (2 Nephi 1:6; emphasis added).

The idiom takes on many forms, one of which is used by Isaiah, who is quoted by Nephi to tell of what God will do with scattered Israel. "And it shall come to pass in that day that the **Lord shall set his hand** again the second time to recover the remnant of his people which shall be left, from Assyria, and from Egypt, and from Pathros, and from Cush, and from Elam, and from Shinar, and from Hamath, and from the islands of the sea" (2 Nephi 21:11; emphasis added). This idiom is found so many times throughout the scriptures that no one should have any doubt as to its message. Even though literal things happen, the figurative expressions tell how we should feel and respond to what is said more than to the literal action.

Isaiah gave the message that the Lord is not weak nor is he prone to not hear his people. Isaiah used idioms to express these ideas. He wrote, "Behold, the **Lord's hand is not shortened**, that it cannot save; neither his ear heavy, that it cannot hear" (Isaiah 59:1; emphasis added). The Lord spoke in similar hyperbole regarding his hand. "And the Lord said unto Moses, Is the **Lord's hand waxed short**? Thou shalt see now whether my word shall come to pass unto thee or not" (Numbers 11:23; emphasis added).

"blast of his nostrils"

When we become angered or distressed, our facial muscles tighten, the nose flattens and the nostrils become perceptively more open and more exposed. Therefore, the nostrils are an indicator or symbol of feelings of anger or displeasure. God at times experiences anger and displeasure as a father of disobedient children. So idioms regarding God's nostrils should be no surprise to us since writers seek to describe God's feelings. What is said is no more literal than is a mortal parent's message to a disobedient child today, who might say, "You're on my black list." One child might say to another, "Dad really blasted me for not doing my homework. He was really breathing fire down on me all night." If we can understand such expressions today, we should be able to catch God's feelings recorded as follows: "By the blast of God they perish, and by the breath of his nostrils are they consumed" (Job 4:9).

Regarding the waters through which the children of Israel escaped the record reports: "And with the blast of thy nostrils the waters were gathered together, the floods stood upright as an heap, and the depths were congealed in the heart of the sea" (Exodus 15:8). A later account described God's help this way: "And the channels of the sea appeared, the foundations of the world were discovered, at the rebuking of the Lord, at the blast of the breath of his nostrils" (2 Samuel 22:16). These idioms describe God's anger and displeasure and what he did just like "with one scribble of his pen, the judge changed everything," expresses an action in our day. Nostrils denote only emotions whereas what is said would come in an expression regarding the mouth such as, "There went up a smoke out of his nostrils, and fire out of his mouth devoured: coals were kindled by it" (2 Samuel 22:9).

Job said of God, "Out of his mouth go burning lamps, and sparks of fire leap out" (Job 41:19). Jeremiah recorded, "Wherefore thus saith the Lord God of hosts, Because ye speak this word, behold, I will make my words in thy mouth fire, and this people wood, and it shall devour them" (Jeremiah 5:14).

Today similar statements are spoken that express strong emotional feelings. Try to identify the idioms used here: "The coach was breathing fire. Nobody dared to even breathe. He had smoke coming out both of his ears, and no one will ever say that he's lost the fire in his belly for the game. That's what sells tickets and keeps other schools knocking on his door."

"thy hand" "thine eye" "thine ear" "thine heart" "thy bowels"

Since God has a body as tangible as a man's, (see D&C 130:22) when we read of his hand, eye, ear, heart, and so forth, we consider it literally. Readers conclude that these body parts seem to be just that—parts of his body. However, the manner in which they are used should alert us as to a figurative use. Jesus spoke several times, "He that hath ears to hear, let him hear" (Matthew 11:15). Everyone has ears, but not everyone listens. We all have eyes, but not everyone sees actions that display feelings and intent or needs. Literally, we can look at someone's hand. But we can figuratively say, "I've seen your hand in many places. You have done more good than most people know about."

While imprisoned for months, Joseph Smith recorded his prayer to God. His dialogue took on the form of questions of request. He was hopeful of deliverance by God from the circumstance to which he and others were subjected. He used the following powerful, and beautiful figurative expressions. He wrote:

> 2 How long shall **thy hand** be stayed, and **thine eye**, yea thy pure eye, behold from the eternal heavens the wrongs of thy people and of thy servants, and **thine ear** be penetrated with their cries?
>
> 4 O Lord God Almighty, maker of heaven, earth, and seas, and of all things that in them are, and who controllest and subjectest the devil, and the dark and benighted dominion of Sheol—stretch forth **thy hand**; let **thine eye** pierce; let thy pavilion be taken up; let thy hiding place no longer be covered; let **thine ear** be inclined; let **thine heart** be softened, and **thy bowels** moved with compassion toward us. (D&C 121:2, 4; emphasis added)

God did hear and see. He extended his hand and Joseph and his associates were eventually freed. One can only imagine the aching of God's heart that some of his children would imprison others and cause them to suffer so much. His bowels, or the very most depths of emotion, must have called out loudly as well, until in his wisdom he chose to soften the hearts of some of the captors so that they would release Joseph and his associates.

Moses recorded that God had given to the people hearts to perceive, eyes to see, and ears to hear (see Deuteronomy 29:4). Such figurative language was used by Jacob. If we had parents who could communicate well, we can possibly catch the meaning of what Jacob said about God and those who were disobedient. He wrote, "O that he would show you that he can pierce you, and with one glance of his eye he can smite you to the dust!" (Jacob 2:15).

The figurative language comes through clearly in these idioms. Does God have a name? Of course he does. Does he have eyes? Of course he does. Even though God has eyes, the message of this verse is about being aware rather than the eyes themselves. "For now have I chosen and sanctified this house, that **my name** may be there for ever: and **mine eyes** and **mine heart** shall be there perpetually" (2 Chronicles 7:16; emphasis added).

Jesus said, "he that hath ears to hear, let him hear." Moses wrote, "Yet the Lord hath not given you a heart to perceive, and eyes to see, and ears to hear, unto his day" (Deuteronomy 29:4). Clearly these phrases are not speaking of actual body parts, but the actions of seeing, hearing, and feeling the truth. Jeremiah spoke the same message in these words, "And I will give you pastors according to mine heart, which shall feed you with knowledge and understanding" (Jeremiah 3:15).

Many children have stated that their mother had "eyes in the back of her head," and that one look from their father told them they were "going to die" for what they had done. Literally, none of this was so. But figuratively it was real!

"footsteps of God"

Where God goes is referred to as "his footsteps." But since that is an idiom, it does not literally tell where he goes. He goes into the hearts and minds of his children, both the righteous and the wicked. The psalmist tried to tell of this metaphoric journey by writing, "Thy way is in the sea, and thy path in the great waters, and thy footsteps are not known" (Psalms 77:19).

The psalmist also tried to depict the evil works of those who castigated the labors of God's anointed. He also wrote, "Wherewith thine enemies have reproached, O Lord; wherewith they have reproached the footsteps of thine anointed" (Psalms 89:51).

The scriptural writings of poetry and prophecy will not be read nor understood well by people who cannot understand figurative language. For some, such a skill comes naturally, but for others, it must be cultured and practiced. Making yourself aware of the challenge is the first step. To know that God speaks and directs figuratively all the time is essential.

> 34 God, Himself spoke the following, "Wherefore, verily I say unto you that all things unto me are spiritual, and not at any time have I given unto you a law which was temporal; neither any man, nor the children of men; neither Adam, your father, whom I created.
>
> 35 Behold, I gave unto him that he should be an agent unto himself; and I gave unto him commandment, but no temporal commandment gave I unto him, for my commandments are spiritual; they are not natural nor temporal, neither carnal nor sensual" (D&C 29:34–35).

Spiritual commands are often communicated in the figurative sense. That is why understanding figurative forms of speech is essential.

"bowels are filled with mercy"

The deepest feelings are described as coming from the most inward place within us—our bowels. Such rich attributes such as mercy are not surface sensations. They come from empathy, compassion, and understanding. Often the holdings, not easily observed, and the sounds of distress or smooth operation, are said to come from the bowels of a ship. They are in the deepest place in the ship, which is neither the deck nor the bridge.

Notice the following description of our Savior's work, "And he will take upon him death, that he may loose the bands of death which bind his people; and he will take upon him their infirmities, that his **bowels may be filled with mercy,** according to the flesh, that he may know according to the flesh how to succor his people according to their infirmities" (Alma 7:12; emphasis added).

Alma also stated, "Now my brethren, we see that God is mindful of every people, whatsoever land they may be in; yea, he numbereth his people, and his **bowels of mercy** are over all the earth. Now this is my joy, and my great thanksgiving; yea, and I will give thanks unto my God forever. Amen" (Alma 26:37; emphasis added).

Isaiah pled with the Lord using the same idiom, "Look down from heaven, and behold from the habitation of thy holiness and of thy glory: where is thy zeal and thy strength, the sounding of **thy bowels and of thy mercies** toward me? are they restrained?" (Isaiah 63:15; emphasis added).

"see my face"

Sight is the sense upon which we so heavily rely for information and validation. When information comes of which we are uncertain, we often say, "Show me." Thomas was not with the other disciples when they witnessed the resurrected Savior. John records, "But Thomas, one of the twelve, called Didymus, was not with them when Jesus came. The other disciples therefore said unto him, We have seen the Lord. But he said unto them, Except I shall see in his hands the print of the nails, and put my finger into the print of the nails, and thrust my hand into his side, I will not believe" (John 20:24–25). Our dependence upon sight, as illustrated by Thomas, is our first choice. It happens because of our very nature. We depend upon it passionately. However, as mentioned earlier, the word *see* has many definitions. Most comprehensive dictionaries list at least eight. Three of the most common are:

1. To perceive by the eye
2. To have experience of—to undergo or to come to know or discover
3. To form a mental picture of—to visualize—to perceive the meaning or importance of—to understand

So when this word appears, our first challenge is to determine which meaning of the word is in play. It is so natural to generally choose the first definition—to perceive by the eye. However, God most often puts significance upon processes that do not include our physical eyes.

In spiritual matters, our greatest assurances are to come through the Holy Spirit. Jesus visited the people of Zarahemla following his resurrection. He appointed twelve disciples there and instructed them with these words: "And again, more blessed are they who shall believe in your words because that ye shall testify that ye have seen me, and that ye know that I am. Yea, blessed are they who shall believe in your words, and come down into the depths of humility and be baptized, for they shall be visited with fire and with the Holy Ghost, and shall receive a remission of their sins" (3 Nephi 12:2).

In 1829, the Lord said the following for the benefit of Oliver Cowdery, "Yea, behold, I will tell you in your mind and in your heart, by the Holy Ghost, which shall come upon you and which shall dwell in your heart. Now, behold, this is the spirit of revelation; behold, this is the spirit by which Moses brought the children of Israel through the Red Sea on dry ground" (D&C 8:2–3). Seeing with the physical eye is not the first and most important medium used by God in telling us truth.

Notice the idioms in the following verse which was spoken by the Lord to Joseph Smith in 1833: "Verily, thus saith the Lord: It shall come to pass that every soul who **forsaketh his sins** and **cometh unto me**, and **calleth on my name**, and **obeyeth my voice**, and **keepeth my commandments**, shall **see my face** and **know that I am**" (D&C 93:1; emphasis added).

Although the highlighted phrases show literal action, they tell much more figuratively. As with phrases like "hold my hand," or "give me a kiss," these phrases do not indicate motive or intensity when taken literally. But as idioms they figuratively tell far more than just the action. Figurative expressions show deeper and richer meaning and purpose. We must do more than just forsake our sins. We must do so because of faith in God. Some may forsake their sins for love, power, or compulsion. People may call on the name of God out of desperation rather than from devotion and worship.

Can a blind person see the face of God? Can a deaf person obey his voice? When selecting which definitions to apply to the word *see*, the proper choice to make would not be the first in a dictionary—to perceive with the eye. The wiser choice would be the second, the third, or a combination of the two. That would suggest to have an experience of, to undergo, or to come to know or discover. It would include to form a mental picture of, to visualize, to perceive the meaning or importance of, to understand.

Next, consider the second element of the idiom. It is the use of the face as the part of the body that is seen. The idiom is not to "see God," but to "see his face." The face is the window in which emotions, sensitivity, and intensity are displayed. The face includes the expression of the eyes, the position of the mouth, the wrinkled brow, and the nose. All combined facets of the face disclose a message that doesn't even need words. Often it is said, "If looks could kill, I'd be dead," or "The look in my mother's eye told me everything I needed to know."

To "see the face" of God is an idiom. It is not the statement telling of visually seeing his face. Naturally, many consider physically and visually seeing God's face as the basis of having a sure witness. However, some have been in the presence of God, seen him, and yet have not believed in him. Thousands saw Jesus in mortality and yet did not gain faith in him. They looked upon his physical face and did not discover or perceive the importance of his life and work. In effect, they did not "see his face."

One of our paramount challenges, according to Joseph Smith, is to know that the course we are pursuing in our life is pleasing to God.[1] Ask yourself the question: "How will I know that I am pleasing to God?" Your answer will be "by seeing his face!" That is the message of this well-used idiom.

John the Revelator recorded in the final summary of his revelation, the "payoff" of those who have overcome the challenges of mortality. He stated:

> 1 And he shewed me a pure river of water of life, clear as crystal, proceeding out of the throne of God and of the Lamb.
>
> 2 In the midst of the street of it, and on either side of the river, was there the tree of life, which bare twelve manner of fruits, and yielded her fruit every month: and the leaves of the tree were for the healing of the nations.
>
> 3 And there shall be no more curse: but the throne of God and of the Lamb shall be in it; and his servants shall serve him:
>
> 4 And **they shall see his face**; and **his name shall be in their foreheads**. (Revelation 22:1-4; emphasis added)

Following the idiom, "shall see his face," is another idiom. They both are beyond the literal. They suggest a level of obedience and devotion that is only limited by commitment, emotions, and feelings. They also indicate possession. Those who have been obedient and believe they have pleased God are made known to all who recognize the name of the Savior, for the second idiom states that his name will be on the most prominent recognition location—the forehead. To identify either of these sayings of Jesus as literal is using poor scriptural judgment. It is just the same as to believe that Jesus meant for us to literally cut off our hands or pluck out our eyes if they were evil. Jesus taught, "And if thy right eye offend thee, **pluck it out**, and cast it from thee: for it is profitable for thee that one of thy members should perish, and not that thy whole body should be cast into hell. And if thy right hand offend thee, cut it off, and **cast it from thee**: for it is profitable for thee that one of thy members should perish, and not that thy whole body should be cast into hell" (Matthew 5:29–30).

These are metaphors. His intention was that if something you are seeing is wrong, quit looking at it. If something you are doing is wrong, stop it. We say to someone doing something they shouldn't do to "cut it out." There is a greater message than just identifying something as being wrong or evil. You must remove it. The message has the same finality as an announcement from an athlete who sees that it is no longer good for him to continue playing a sport competitively. So, he says that he is going to "hang up his cleats." We also communicate our intentions to never return to certain pursuits, not places, when we say that "we have burned all our bridges" regarding a relationship or practice. We "sell all that [we have]," (Luke 18:22) and we "turn over a new leaf."

"my back parts"

The opposite of seeing God's face is to see his back parts. God spoke to Moses after the terrible disobedience of the people at Sinai. The people lost the privilege of having their leader be blessed with seeing God's face. God said, "And I will take away mine hand, and thou shalt see my back parts: but my face shall not be seen" (Exodus 33:23). The people at Sinai had disappointed God immensely and their standing with God was the issue at hand. A modern action of this is to literally turn your back to someone with whom you are speaking or to just say, "I turn my back on everything you are doing." What Moses was going to be able to see or not see was only an indicator of his people's relationship with their God. A sight or sound can be a huge indicator of approval or disapproval as illustrated by idioms used today. "I'd give anything just to smell my mother's hair again." "I wish like anything I could hear my dad just call me by name once more."

"make bare his arm" 1 Nephi 22:10

One of the expressions the Lord has used to figuratively express his intentions is to state that he would "make bare his arm." The arm is considered the symbol of power and strength. And when God states that he will make bare his arm, he is saying that his power will be seen, that it can be observed, if people will only look. Nephi wrote: "And I would, my brethren, that ye should know that all the kindreds of the earth cannot be blessed unless he shall make bare his arm in the eyes of the nations. Wherefore, the Lord God will proceed to make bare his arm in the eyes of all the nations, in bringing about his covenants and his gospel unto those who are of the house of Israel." (1 Nephi 22:10–11)

- Question: To whom will he make bare his arm?
- Answer: He will make bare his arm in the eyes of the nations.

- Question: What will the nations see?
- Answer: They will be shown the covenants and his Gospel.

- Question: Will God show his arm literally?
- Answer: Of course not. His covenants and his gospel will be taught and revealed by his servants.

- Question: Who are his servants?
- Answer: They are prophets and missionaries. The Lord spoke to those who were to redeem the lands they lost in Missouri that they should make bare his arm (see D&C 109:51).

- Question: When the nations see the arm of the Lord, what will they see?
- Answer: Section 133 of the Doctrine and Covenants is the Lord's response to the many things which the Elders desired to know concerning the preaching the Gospel to the inhabitants of the earth. Joseph Smith was instructed by the Lord:

> 3 For **he shall make bare his holy arm in the eyes of all the nations**, and all the ends of **the earth shall see the salvation of their God**.
>
> 4 Wherefore, [1] **prepare ye**, prepare ye, O my people; [2] **sanctify yourselves**; [3] **gather ye together**, O ye people of my church, upon the land of Zion, all you that have not been commanded to tarry.
>
> 5 [4] **Go ye out from Babylon.** [5] **Be ye clean** that bear the vessels of the Lord.
>
> 6 [6] **Call your solemn assemblies**, and [7] **speak often one to another.** [8] **And let every man call upon the name of the Lord.** (D&C 133:3–6, emphasis and structure added)

That is how the arm of the Lord will be made bare.

- Question: What if people do not see the Lord's arm?
- Answer: "And the arm of the Lord shall be revealed; and the day cometh that they who will not hear the voice of the Lord, neither the voice of his servants, neither give heed to the words of the prophets and apostles, shall be cut off from among the people" (D&C 1:14).
  - "But before the arm of the Lord shall fall, an angel shall sound his trump, and the saints that have slept shall come forth to meet me in the cloud" (D&C 45:45).
  - "Then shall the arm of the Lord fall upon the nations" (D&C 45:47).
  - "And then cometh the day when the arm of the Lord shall be revealed in power in convincing the nations, the heathen nations, the house of Joseph, of the gospel of their salvation" (D&C 90:10).

I hope the arm of the Lord has been made bare to each one of us, that we know of his covenants made with Israel and how salvation will come to his children.

"healing in his wings" Malachi 4:2

This phrase is very familiar to all Christians. It is included in the second verse of the Christmas carol "Hark the Herald Angels Sing."

2nd verse:
Hail the heav'n born Prince of Peace!
Hail the Son of Righteousness!
Light and life to all he brings,
Ris'n **with healing in his wings**.
Mild he lays his glory by,
Born that man no more may die;
Born to raise the sons of earth,
Born to give them second birth.
Hark! the herald angels sing
Glory to the newborn King![2]

It also is included in the Latter-day hymn written by LaVonne VanOrden, "Come, O thou King of Kings."

1st verse:
Come, O thou King of Kings!
We've waited long for thee,
With **healing in thy wings**
To set thy people free.
Come, thou desire of nations, come;
Let Israel now be gathered home.[3]

The phrase is recorded in scripture in Malachi 4:2, "But unto you that fear my name shall the **Sun of righteousness** arise with **healing in his wings**." The interpretation of Malachi's words are opined by scholars because the spelling of "Sun of righteousness." Martin Luther leaned toward a significance of the word *sun* as opposed to *son*. He saw it as an indirect reference to the Savior. Others since have doubted its direct reference to the Messiah at all. The NIV (New Inspired Version) adds to the confusion. The same verse reads, "But for you who revere my name, the sun of righteousness will rise with healing in its wings." Notice that not only is the word *sun* not capitalized, but the NIV uses the impersonal pronoun "its" to modify whose wings are being spoken of. Some feel that Malachi was not making reference to Jehovah, but to the sun in the heavens.

For those who read the Book of Mormon, all doubt regarding the name Son of Righteousness disappears by reading two separate verses from two sources. The first reads: "Behold, they will crucify **him**; and after he is laid in a sepulchre for the space of three days he shall rise from the dead, **with healing in his wings**; and all those who shall believe on his name shall be saved in the kingdom of God. Wherefore, my soul delighteth to prophesy concerning him, for I have seen his day, and my heart doth magnify his holy name" (2 Nephi 25:13; emphasis added).

The second verse contains the words of the resurrected Lord himself as he visited the righteous Nephites and said, "But unto you that fear my name, shall the **Son of Righteousness** arise with healing in **his** wings" (3 Nephi 25:2; emphasis added).

All apprehension is gone regarding who the Son of Righteousness is and how his name should be spelled in Malachi. However, the question emerges, and we ask, "What are his wings"? Let us be taught by Matthew in his gospel. He tells of a woman who had a blood disorder.

We must remember that Matthew was always trying to show in his writing that Jesus was the fulfillment of messianic prophecy. Jehovah spoke to Israel, "for I am the Lord that healeth thee" (Exodus 15:26). Moses spoke of Jehovah, "And the Lord will take away from thee all sickness" (Deuteronomy 7:15). David testified that the Lord is one "Who forgiveth all iniquities; who healeth all thy diseases" (Psalms 103:3). Jeremiah testified for the Lord to the outcasts of Judah, "For I will restore health unto thee and I will heal thee of thy wounds" (Jeremiah 30:17). So Matthew may not be just including in his gospel account a mere incident in the ministry of the Savior. He recounts:

> 20 And, behold, a woman, which was diseased with an issue of blood twelve years, came behind him, and **touched the hem** of his garment:
>
> 21 For she said within herself, If I may but touch his garment, I shall be whole.
>
> 22 But Jesus turned him about, and when he saw her, he said, Daughter, be of good comfort; thy faith hath made thee whole. And the woman was made whole from that hour. (Matthew 9:20–22; emphasis added).

Later Matthew adds:

> 34 And when they were gone over, they came into the land of Gennesaret.
>
> 35 And when the men of that place had knowledge of him, they sent out into all that country round about, and brought unto him all that were diseased;
>
> 36 And besought him that they might only **touch the hem** of his garment: and as many as touched were made perfectly whole (Matthew 14:34–36; emphasis added).

These accounts along with others by Matthew show fulfillment of Jesus being the messiah who would heal; but what about that phrase "with healing in his wings?" Reading the Bible Dictionary regarding "hem of garment" becomes wonderfully helpful.

> An important part of an Israelite's dress, owing to the regulation of Num 15:38–39. It was really a tassel at each "wing" or corner of the *tallith* or mantle (Matt 14:36). The law required that it should be bound with a thread of blue, the color of heaven. The strict Jews to this day wear these tassels, though they are usually concealed. The Pharisees

made them conspicuously large (Matt 23:5). It would be the tassel that hung over the shoulder at the back that the woman with the issue of blood came and touched (Luke 8:44; also Exodus 28:33–34).[4]

The Savior followed rabbinical laws and would have worn the tallith. This mantle, square in form, was folded diagonally and worn over or from the head or shoulders like a large scarf. Two of the corners hung outward off the shoulders and over the arms, which if extended, let the tallith take on the semblance of "wings." From this comes the wonderful phrase **"with healing in his wings."** Truly the Savior came with healing in his wings. There was power in the office of high priest and rabbi which he held. Such power was not in the wings of the other priests of his day. That was the testimony of Matthew and Luke as they recorded the story of the woman who had suffered for twelve years with her condition. She wasn't just reaching for any part of any clothing Jesus was wearing. She believed he was the Messiah! That's why she testified that she knew if she could only touch the hem of his prayer shawl (his wing) she could be healed. She believed he was divine and had the power to heal—just as the woman at the well came to believe the Savior was the source of living water. This understanding likely will not change one's faith in the Savior's power to heal, but appreciating the phrase adds richness to our understanding of the language of God and his prophets.

Notes

1. See Joseph Smith, *Lectures on Faith*, (Salt Lake City: Deseret Book, 1985), Lecture 6.
2. "Hark the Herald Angels Sing," *Hymns* no. 209.
3. "Come O Thou King of Kings," *Hymns* no. 59.
4. See Bible Dictionary, "Hem of garment,", 700.

IDIOMS SPOKEN BY MODERN PROPHETS

The prophets of our own day use language forms of every type and kind, including idioms. Idioms often appear in the titles of conference addresses as well as in the text of their remarks. Some examples of idioms used in remarks by prophets are found in the following quotes:

- "Let us have integrity and not write checks with our tongues which our conduct cannot cash."[1]
- "The bullet-torn flesh fertilized the soil; the blood they shed moistened the seed; and the spirits they sent heaven-ward will testify against them throughout eternities. The cause persists and grows." Elder Spencer W. Kimball said, speaking of the sacrifice of Joseph Smith and those who took his life.[2]
- "If certain mortal experiences were cut short, it would be like pulling up a flower to see how the roots are doing. Put another way, too many anxious openings of the oven door, and the cake falls instead of rising. . . . Endurance is more than pacing up and down within the cell of our circumstance; it is not only acceptance of things allotted to us, it is to 'act for ourselves' by magnifying what is allotted to us."[3]
- "It is difficult to resist when your peers are pulling you down into the swamp of narcotics. It takes steel in your spine to say no."[4]

- Elder Neal A. Maxwell wrote:

To those who mean well but thoughtlessly speak of 'building a better relationship' with God (which sounds like a transaction between mortals desiring reciprocity), it needs to be said that our relationship with God is already established in a genealogical sense. Perhaps what such individuals intend to say is that we must draw closer to God. But we are to worship, to adore, and to obey God, not build a better relationship with Him.

There is an attitudinal and behavioral bridge that we need to build in order for us to draw closer to Him, and thus be ready to return Home—*cum laude* or *summa cum laude*—to receive of His loving fullness. We must want to do this more than we want to do anything else. Otherwise, even if we avoid wickedness, our journey will end in the suburbs, somewhere short of the City of God.[5]

- "Do I worship the 'scriptural Christ' or just the traditional and commercial? Do I know more than the 'story?' "[6]
- "That we may have the wisdom and determination to cross the bridges the Savior built for each of us is my sincere prayer."[7]
- "It is my firm belief that if as individual people, as families, communities, and nations, we could, like Peter, fix our eyes on Jesus, we too might walk triumphantly over the 'swelling waves of disbelief' and remain 'unterrified amid the rising winds of doubt.' "[8]
- "You will meet Goliaths who threaten you. Whether your Goliath is a town bully or is the temptation to steal or to destroy or the temptation to rob or the desire to curse and swear; if your Goliath is the desire to wantonly destroy or the temptation to lust and to sin, or the urge to avoid activity, whatever is your Goliath, he can be slain. But remember, to be the victor, one must follow the path that David followed."[9]

If anyone doubts the use of figurative idiomatic use by modern prophets, read their talks given in general conference or other settings. Or next general conference, list or tally the figurative expressions. To some, the number of idioms used will come as no surprise. For others, a new appreciation for this language form may build.

Notes

1. Neal A. Maxwell, BYU Devotional, 10 October 1978.
2. Conference Report, Apr. 1955, 96.
3. Neal A. Maxwell, "Endure It Well," *Ensign*, May 1990, 34.
4. Gordon B. Hinckley, "A Plague on the World," *New Era*, Jul. 1990, 4.
5. Neal A. Maxwell, *All These Things Shall Give Thee Experience*, (Salt Lake City: Deseret Book, 1980), 3.
6. Bruce R. McConkie, Fireside address at BYU, September 5, 1976.
7. Thomas S. Monson, "The Bridge Builder," *Ensign*, Nov. 2003, 67.
8. Howard W. Hunter, "The Beacon in the Harbor of Peace," *Ensign*, Nov. 1992, 18.
9. Spencer W. Kimball, "The Davids and the Goliaths," *Ensign*, Nov. 1974, 82.

IDIOMS USED IN THE HYMNS OF THE CHURCH

Since music deals so much with feelings and passion, we should expect to find figurative language in almost every hymn that is sung in the Church. The hymns we sing in worship are indeed replete with idioms. Some hymns are titled with an idiom. Others contain idioms within the verses. They are so familiar to us that we often do not notice the phrases for what they are, nor do we assess the power they project. Many hymns are intended to move us to action. Some make comparisons to objects of power and strength, while others cause us to think of tenderness and virtue.

The following are a few hymns, familiar to most of us, that have idioms within their titles. There are many more than these listed here. And, if the title has at least one idiom within it, it's likely there are more within its lyrics.

"A Mighty Fortress Is Our God"	Hymn 68
"Be Still, My Soul"	Hymn 124
"Beautiful Zion, Built Above"	Hymn 44
"Come unto Jesus"	Hymn 117
"Each Life That Touches Ours for Good"	Hymn 293
"Firm as the Mountains Around Us . . ."	Hymn 255
"God Speed the Right"	Hymn 106
"High on the Mountain Top"	Hymn 5

"You Can Make the Pathway Bright"	Hymn 228
"Israel, Israel, God Is Calling"	Hymn 7
"Jesus, Savior, Pilot Me"	Hymn 104
"Lead, Kindly Light"	Hymn 97
"Let Us All Press On"	Hymn 243
"Put Your Shoulder to the Wheel"	Hymn 252
"Scatter Sunshine"	Hymn 230
"We Are Sowing"	Hymn 216
"Sweet Is the Work"	Hymn 147
"Teach Me to Walk in the Light"	Hymn 304
"The Lord Is My Light"	Hymn 89
"There Is Sunshine in My Soul Today"	Hymn 227
"Who's on the Lord's Side?"	Hymn 260

Why do we say good-bye when parting? Research into the word or phrase was done by those who wrote the hymn, "God Be with You Till We Meet Again."[1] The word *good-bye* is short for "God Be With You"[2]

"Balm of Gilead"

The hymn titled "Did You Think to Pray"[3] can likely be sung by most members of the Church by memory. The third verse contains an idiom, which very few understand, yet they have sung it hundreds of times. The reason it is not understood is that its origin is obscure. The idiom is "Balm of Gilead." What does it mean?

When the children of Israel came up out of Egypt to possess the land of Canaan, they first encountered the Land of Gilead on the east side of the Jordan River. Eventually the tribes of Gad and Manasseh, were assigned this land as their inheritance. There was a small tree or large bush from which they removed a moist substance from under its skin or bark, which they used as a balm or ointment. This balm was helpful in healing their wounds. It was called "the balm of Gilead." However, they used it so much that the plant became extinct.

Even though the plant has not existed for thousands of years, an old spiritual song says, "There is a balm in Gilead!" The words of the song tell that Jesus is now the Balm in Gilead. He, today, is the balm to heal the sin-sick soul.

Chorus:
There is a balm in Gilead,
To make the wounded whole,
There is a balm in Gilead,
To heal the sin sick soul.

1st verse:
Some times I feel discouraged
And think my work's in vain,
And then the Holy Spirit
Revives my soul again.

2nd verse:
If you cannot sing like angels,
If you cannot preach like Paul,
You can tell the love of Jesus,
And say, "He died for all."[4]

So the next time you sing the hymn, "Did You Think to Pray?" and you sing the lyrics, "Balm of Gilead did you borrow?" I hope you will think about the healing traits and powers of the Savior. If you don't, then you have "missed the boat."

"restoring their judges"

Those who know the stories told in the Book of Judges probably wonder why the lives of some who failed miserably in judging properly are included in the Book of the Judges. Most prominent among these was Sampson, but also leaders such as Abimelech and Ibzan who displayed very poor judgment. So why are they in the Book of Judges? The answer comes because of knowing that the Hebrew word translated as judge was not a good translation choice. A more accurate translation would have been "deliverer" or "savior." So these people in the Book of Judges are there not for their great judgment. They are there because God intended them to deliver or save Israel from their enemies through their leadership. This intention by the Lord is recorded: "Nevertheless the Lord raised up judges, which delivered them out of the hand of those that spoiled them" (Judges 2:16).

The phrase "restoring their judges" is not scriptural, but was used by William W. Phelps in the hymn that was written and used at the dedication of the Kirtland Temple in 1836. This hymn is entitled "The Spirit of God."[5]

1ˢᵗ verse:
The Spirit of God like a fire is burning
The latter-day glory begins to come forth.
The visions and blessings of old are returning
And angels are coming to visit the earth.

2ⁿᵈ verse:
The Lord is extending the Saint's understanding,
Restoring their judges and all as at first.
The knowledge and power of God are expanding;
The veil o'er the earth is beginning to burst.

The message of the phrase "restoring their judges" would be clearer if we applied the message of the Book of Judges where the Lord is giving deliverers and saviors to us as a people again. Joseph Smith and others certainly were exactly that. Some proved themselves to be just like those in the Book of Judges and did not demonstrate the attributes to be deliverers or saviors, but proved faithless and misleading. Of course, deliverers and saviors can only perform such acts if they make good judgments.

In this same light and manner, many expect bishops to make judgments for them since each bishop is called as a "judge in Israel" when called as a bishop (D&C 107:72). Some see this calling only with an eye for the judging part and not the delivering and saving mission they perform. Sometimes Saints struggle if a bishop's counsel is not what they deem good judgment. They expect, since he has been set apart as a "judge in Israel," to receive pleasing advice and counsel from him. They do not realize that saving or delivering us might need to come because we need to learn something that will save or deliver us. The objective of such action may not be apparent at the time in the same manner Naaman did not understand God's command given by Elijah to dip himself in the waters of the Jordan River. The judgment of a bishop may take the form of requested repentance or a change with which the offender may not agree. However, time generally bears out the judgment of such an officer. The message of "restoring their judges" expresses once again that the Lord has restored saviors and deliverers after a long period of darkness. No wonder the chorus of Phelps' hymn includes, "We'll sing and we'll shout." There is great reason to be excited and joyful!

Notes

1. "God Be With You Till We Meet Again" *Hymns* no. 152.
2. Music and the Spoken Word, Jan. 29, 2006.
3. "Did You Think to Pray," *Hymns*, no. 140.
4. "There is a Balm in Gilead," traditional song.
5. "The Spirit of God," *Hymns* no. 2.

Idioms Regarding Church Practices

"clapped his hands upon all them"

While preaching at the Waters of Mormon, Alma suggested that those who believed his preaching could be baptized. It is recorded, "And now when the people had heard these words, they clapped their hands for joy, and exclaimed: This is the desire of our hearts" (Mosiah 18:11). There seems to be little confusion as to what the people did in response to their positive feelings—they clapped. However, later in the Book of Mormon account of Alma preaching to the Zoramites, another expression is recorded regarding something Alma did. The account states: "Now it came to pass that when Alma had said these words, that he **clapped his hands upon all them** who were with him. And behold, as he clapped his hands upon them, they were filled with the Holy Spirit" (Alma 31:36; emphasis added).

What did he do? And is what he did a part of Church procedure today? To answer this question, we must ask the ever-present question: Is what we read literal or figurative? The answer to this question regarding the first verse quoted seems to be literal—they clapped their hands together as they did in 2 Kings 11:12. However, the verse in

Alma 31 includes an idiom. Many words have more than one meaning, especially when moving into the realm of figurative expression. For example, you might say, "They are going to walk all over me." Is that literal or figurative? It could be either, and the question will be answered by reading the full account and knowing the meanings, figurative and literal of "walk all over me." The same is true for the words "clapped his hands." In addition to clap meaning "to applaud," it also means "to put, move or set firmly." So Alma placed (clapped) his hands firmly (with power) upon those who believed, and they were filled with the Holy Ghost. This is a wonderful manner in which to describe the process of what Alma did. With just that one action word, the idea of power, the idea of change, and the idea of permanence are all projected. This ordinance is practiced in the Church today. However, the idiom is seldom used to describe what really takes place.

Alma's use of the verb clapped is not unparalleled in idiomatic language. Most people recognize what it means if they are told of a criminal who was arrested and "they clapped him in irons." The word *clapped* suggests that it was done with power and its effect was firm. The word *clap* suggests firmness so much that a sexually transmitted disease was named "clap." Once you got it, it was difficult to be free from it. It was given this simple nickname in the days before most antibiotics were developed, which now give relief and help control the infection. Reference is now seldom made to the condition by its former name of "clap."

"cast out"

This idiom has basically one meaning but numerous applications. Therefore, we should be certain not to apply it improperly. The basic message of the phrase is to "put from you," or to "separate away from." Devils were to be "cast out." Salt that has lost its savor will be "cast out."

However, regarding the Church, the Lord gave a revelation regarding the law of the Church. This revelation, simply known as "The Law," records the reasons for which a person should be separated from membership in the Church. "Thou shalt not steal; and he that stealeth and will not repent shall be cast out" (D&C 42:20). Similar words follow for those unrepentant who commit lying, lust, adultery, and murder. The Lord further states: "Thou knowest my laws concerning these things are given in my scriptures; he that sinneth and repenteth not shall be cast out. . . . And it shall come to pass, that he that sinneth and repenteth not shall be cast out of the church, and shall not receive again that which he has consecrated unto the poor and the needy of my church, or in other words, unto me—" (D&C 42:28, 37). Just because we are cast out from the Church, does not mean that we are cast out from the Lord. However, there will come a time when the wicked and unrepentant will be separated from those obedient to God, and they will be then cast out following the final judgment.

"gave forth their lots"

Following the suicide of Judas, the apostles needed to fill the vacancy in the Quorum of the Twelve Apostles. The account reads as follows, "And they **gave forth their lots**; and the lot fell upon Matthias; and he was numbered with the eleven apostles" (Acts 1:26; emphasis added).

Many interpret this verse with the idea that they had an election. However, consider how the idiom is likewise used today in the following examples: "It became my lot as the oldest brother to care for my siblings." "Since I had the combination, it was my lot to open the vault." One's lot has more to do with assignment or place than it does with gaming.

There are no elections in the Church even though the idiom "cast lots" may be used. The idiom may likewise be used outside of the Church without elections being held. Today someone may say, "I cast my lot and chose my family over that job."

Zacharias was told by an angel, that his barren wife, Elizabeth, would conceive and bear a son. This son would be the forerunner for the Messiah. Zacharias had been given the duty of entering into the Holy of Holies on the Day of Atonement at the temple. The event is recorded in these words, "According to the custom of the priest's office, **his lot** was to burn incense when he went into the temple of the Lord" (Luke 1:9; emphasis added). In the Church, casting lots and giving lots, have to do with duty, not elections.

"was ordained"

The word *ordain* has a much broader meaning in the King James Bible than it does in the Book of Mormon and latter-day revelation.

It is felt in modern church terminology to involve a formal ceremony wherein someone receives the priesthood or an office within the priesthood. This is not the case in the Bible. There it means to proclaim, declare, designate, determine, decree, or appoint. Consider what was said regarding the filling of the vacancy created by the death of Judas in the Twelve. "Beginning from the baptism of John, unto that same day that he was taken up from us, must one **be ordained** to be a witness with us of his resurrection" (Acts 1:22; emphasis added). Later Matthias was called and surely he was formally ordained to the apostleship (v. 26); however that is not the intent of the phrase "be ordained" in the verse cited.

Peter in his first recorded speech to the Gentiles tells that he and others were commanded to testify that Jesus Christ was ordained. Peter said, "And he commanded us to preach unto the people, and to testify that it is he which **was ordained** of God to be the Judge of quick and dead" (Acts 10:42; emphasis added).

For those of us who have observed, participated in, and respected a formal ordination, it is a little difficult to let go of the narrow interpretation of the word *ordain*, but it must be done if the meaning of the writer is to be understood. Paul and Barnabas had success preaching the message that Christ was a messenger of salvation to them as well as to those of Abrahams's children. It was recorded, "And when the Gentiles heard this, they were glad, and glorified the word of the Lord: and as many as **were ordained** to eternal life believed" (Acts 13:48; emphasis added).

With this broader view of the word *ordained* in mind, and also recognizing that "was ordained" is an expression denoting such ideas as "declaring," "designating," and "appointing," a statement attributed to Joseph Smith should be considered. He said, "Every man who has a calling to minister to the inhabitants of the world **was ordained** to that very purpose in the Grand Council of Heaven before this world was."[1] Some choose to use the narrow meaning of the word *ordain* to apply to what the prophet said. However, a wiser choice would be the same usage as that in the Bible and in the broader definition of the word. He would not have been stating that every man had hands laid on his head and thereby was ordained, but instead he would have been teaching that each man was designed, designated, or appointed to receive the priesthood.

"gift of tongues"

This idiom is included among the list of gifts by the apostle Paul as well as in the 7th Article of Faith. Within the doctrines of the Christian churches, belief varies due to the interpretation of the meaning of the idiom. However, Joseph Smith made it clear as to the meaning of the term, its origin, and its expected use. He said, "Tongues were given for the purpose of preaching among those whose language is not understood; as on the day of Pentecost, etc., and it is not necessary for tongues to be taught to the Church particularly, for any man that has the Holy Ghost, can speak of the things of God in his own tongue as well as to speak in another; for faith comes not by signs, but by hearing the word of God."[2]

Clearly, this gift is to be used in the Church. For how else will those who do not speak the same language hear the word of God? Just as on the day of Pentecost, the account says, "And they were all filled with the Holy Ghost, and began to speak with other tongues, as the Spirit gave them utterance" (Acts 2:4).

It is difficult for those who speak English today as their first language to fathom the challenges regarding language that faced the early church. Today if you speak English, it is expected that everyone in the United States, Canada, England, and Australia, in addition to many other nations, will understand you. However, in the day of the New Testament Church, Aramaic, Hebrew, and Greek were all spoken in Palestine. Furthermore, there was a dialect of the Aramaic spoken in the north and another spoken in the south. Among the people who had come to Jerusalem on the day of Pentecost, there were many Jews and Galileans who spoke both dialects. Peter spoke several Aramaic dialects. He had traveled three years with Jesus in Judea, Syria, and other parts of Palestine. There was a need for understanding one another unlike what we experience today. In most societies, one interpreter is sufficient to translate the language being spoken into the language of the hearers. However, there are other countries today which have several dialects to deal with. The gift of tongues is a gift for which Saints pray and experience when the same language is not known by all.

"strong drinks"

The Lord chose this designation for substances from which the Saints should abstain, saying that they were not for the belly, but for the washing of the body (see D&C 89:7). He did not specify in the revelation what was meant by the idiom. It needs definition just like "strong medicine;" "strong action;" "strong advice;" or "strong person."

Understanding what is meant by the idiom requires a historical setting for its origin. Such is provided by Elder James E. Talmage. He explained the meaning of strong drinks as an expression used in the Word of Wisdom in the following language:

> It is evident from a studious reading of the Word of Wisdom and other early revelations in the present dispensation, that the Lord used the language common to the time, such as would be understood without question by the people directly addressed. In the revelation under consideration we read: 'Strong drinks are not for the belly, but for the washing of your bodies'; and the plain meaning is that alcohol in any combination or mixture is injurious to the body when taken internally but may be good for external application. Alcohol in an unmixed state was in that early day no common commodity, and in fact was scarcely known except to the chemist. The ordinary name for liquids containing alcohol was 'strong drinks', and a plainer designation would have been hard to find.[3]

"hot drinks"

This idiom included in the Word of Wisdom (see D&C 89:9), needed definition for the saints in 1833, and still rouses questions today. So an explanation from the time of origin for the phrase is helpful. According to Joel H. Johnson, five months after the Word of Wisdom was revealed, Joseph Smith asked a congregation, "Now, what do we drink when we take our meals? Tea and coffee. Is it not?" Answering his own question, he said, "They are what the Lord meant when he said 'Hot drinks." Hyrum Smith and Brigham Young also defined hot drinks as tea and coffee, explaining that these two stimulants were the hot beverages that were most popular among Americans when the revelation was received.[4]

The literal temperature of the drink originally was a defining element. However, such beverages as iced tea have been included within the designation of "hot drinks" by leaders of the Church since the revelation was given. Changes in similar idioms depend on the era and culture speaking phrases such as, "That's a cool drink;" "That's a hot car;" "That's a cool hot tub;" or "I've got a hot date tonight." Idioms need to be defined and redefined since they are not literal and do not fit all languages and groups the same way.

"they are to be used sparingly"

Regarding the use of flesh of animals and fowls as food, the Lord spoke, "Yea, flesh also of beasts and of the fowls of the air, I, the Lord, have ordained for the use of man with thanksgiving; nevertheless **they are to be used sparingly**" (D&C 89:12; emphasis added). What does "sparingly" mean? God had, previous to this revelation, given several directions regarding the use of meat. His command to Adam and Eve was that they were to have dominion over all creatures. The entire history contained in scripture tells of the flesh of creatures being eaten by God's people. Paul wrote to Timothy and spoke against those who taught that they should abstain from meats. He said that such a person was not ordained of God (see 1 Timothy 4:3). The same decree was given by the Lord in the latter-days. The Lord instructed, "And whoso forbiddeth to abstain from meats, that man should not eat the same, is not ordained of God" (D&C 49:18). So clearly, meats are to be used. But the conditions under which they are to be used generally is the question, and it arises because of the verse that follows the idiom "they are to be used sparingly." The Lord continued, "And it is pleasing unto me that they should not be used, only in times of winter, or of cold, or famine" (D&C 89:13).

So now there seems to be contradiction between instructions the Lord has given. Are meats only to be used in times of winter, cold, or famine? In resolving this question, historical information regarding verse 13 needs to be considered. The Doctrine and Covenants was first published in 1833 under the title, *A Book of Commandments for the Government of the Church of Christ*. Just as this printing was coming off the press, a mob destroyed the printing operation with most of its contents. Only a few copies of unbound pages were heroically saved. Two years later, a second edition was published, containing additional revelations that the first edition did not contain. It was published under the title, Doctrine and Covenants of the Church of Christ. This printing contained section 89, which included the verses and idiom in question. The printer's manuscript for this 1835 Doctrine and Covenants of the Church of Christ has not been found. The manuscript volume "Kirtland Revelations," now in the Church Historian's Library, however, contains a number of the revelations from that printing. In addition, it bears some corrections, in the handwriting of Joseph Smith which are consistent with the 1835 Doctrine and Covenants, as well as the notation "To go into the covenants" by a few of the revelations. His notation regarding the covenants, referred to the volume known as the Doctrine and Covenants. One of those corrections made by Joseph was very small, but it gives a complete reversal to the definition of "they are to be used sparingly."

Joseph deleted one of the commas in verse 13. He made it to read, "And it is pleasing unto me that they should not be used only in times of winter, or of cold, or famine." Notice the absence of a comma between the words *used* and *only*. Removing this comma changes completely the direction from the Lord and puts it in harmony with all the other instructions he has revealed on the subject.

Now you ask, "Why does our present day revelation still contain the comma?" The answer comes from reconstructing historical facts of the time. The Saints were forced to leave Kirtland and gather in Missouri, where they were under severe persecution and oppression. Joseph was imprisoned first in 1837, then again in 1838 until April of 1839. He was reunited with the saints in the last of April. The majority of the Saints were now located on land they had purchased in Illinois and Iowa. He had many matters, large and small, which urgently needed his attention. Members of the Twelve left on missions to England, taking with them personal copies of the 1835 edition of the Doctrine and Covenants and the Book of Mormon. When converts in Europe wanted copies of those volumes of scripture, they were reprinted in England. This process continued until the death of Joseph in 1844 and beyond until 1876. The removal of the comma, eliminated by Joseph, never made its way into the verse. It still appears there today. It allows confusion to those who do not know the background of the verse and to those who desire a change in the accepted practice of the Church regarding the use of meats. The Lord's instructions to the Saints in 1831 regarding eating meats, as well as all other foods, stands as the most clear of all statements. It states;

> 16 Verily I say, that inasmuch as ye do this, the fulness of the earth is yours, the beasts of the field and the fowls of the air, and that which climbeth upon the trees and walketh upon the earth;
> 17 Yea, and the herb, and the good things which come of the

earth, whether for food or for raiment, or for houses, or for barns, or for orchards, or for gardens, or for vineyards;

18 Yea, all things which come of the earth, in the season thereof, are made for the benefit and the use of man, both to please the eye and to gladden the heart;

19 Yea, for food and for raiment, for taste and for smell, to strengthen the body and to enliven the soul.

20 And it pleaseth God that he hath given all these things unto man; for unto this end were they made to be used, with judgment, not to excess, neither by extortion. (D&C 59:16–20; emphasis added)

If one chooses to abstain from eating meats and does so because of personal reasons, that is far apart from believing that God has instructed that meats should be eaten sparingly, and then only in times of winter or famine. The verse in Doctrine and Covenants, section 89, in question, is the only verse which seemingly instructs such limited use of meats. And now upon further examination and clarification of the verse, it does not limit, but encourages the use of meats just like all other scriptural statements given by the Lord through the prophets.

"run and not be weary"

The final verses of the revelation known as "the Word of Wisdom," section 89, include phrases that are clearly idioms. These idioms are many times treated as literal statements and are often used to support stories of superhuman abilities that result from obeying the warnings within the revelation. This is confusing to some who never have partaken of any disallowed food or drink, but yet find themselves suffering from health issues that make them physically inept. The key verse reads, "And shall **run and not be weary**, and shall **walk and not faint**" (D&C 89:20; emphasis added).

Every person who runs experiences weariness from long exertion. Likewise, it is rare that anyone faints from merely walking. Consequently, it is evident that these promises apply more to the things of the Spirit, as we run the race of life. Isaiah was not speaking of God's physical endurance when he said, "for the Lord . . . fainteth not, neither is weary" (see Isaiah 40:28–31).

Clearly the idioms are referencing our "walk through life" and about "running the race" mentioned metaphorically by the Apostle Paul. They are about having the strength and stamina to go through the sprints as well as the long difficult walks of life. Those with no legs, or those confined to wheelchairs, must also run and finish this race.

Notes

1. Joseph Fielding Smith, *Teachings of the Prophet Joseph Smith*, (Salt Lake City: Deseret Book, 1977), 365.
2. Joseph Smith, *History of The Church of Jesus Christ of Latter-day Saints* (Salt Lake City: Deseret News, 1904), 379.
3. *Improvement Era*, 20, 1917, 555.
4. "The Word of Wisdom," *Times and Seasons*, 1 Jun. 1842, 800.

IDIOMS REGARDING ACTS IN NATURE

"wax strong"

The Lord admonished "Let thy bowels also be full of charity towards all men, and to the household of faith, and let virtue garnish thy thoughts unceasingly; then shall thy confidence **wax strong** in the presence of God; and the doctrine of the priesthood shall distil upon thy soul as the dews from heaven" (D&C 121:45; emphasis added). Waxing and waning are terms used to indicate increasing or diminishing and usually refer to the phases of the moon. We call a moon that is becoming larger each night until it is full a "waxing moon." A moon that is decreasing in size we call a "waning moon. So when the Lord tells us that our confidence will "**wax strong** in the presence of God," we should expect to experience an increase in our confidence before God.

The impression of increasing should be associated with those righteous who will inherit the earth as a habitation. The Lord promised, "And the earth shall be given unto them for an inheritance; and they shall multiply and **wax strong**, and their children shall grow up without sin unto salvation" (D&C 45:58; emphasis added). "Waxing strong" was described in the same manner in numerous other verses such as: 4 Nephi 1:40; 3 Nephi 1:29; 3 Nephi 2:3; and Mosiah 9:11.

"end of the world"

Sometimes we do not have to determine or define certain expressions. We only have to be aware of all God has said about them. "The end of the world" is one of those. With only the account found in most versions of the Bible, it is very natural to conclude that this phrase designates a time when this world or earth will end. Since God has warned about great destructions and calamities, they are often associated with such an event. However, Joseph Smith changed or added to the verse most often quoted relative to this subject. The King James version states, "And as he sat upon the mount of Olives, the disciples came unto him privately, saying, Tell us, when shall these things be? and what shall be the sign of thy coming, and of the **end of the world**?" (Matthew 24:3; emphasis added). Joseph Smith identifies what the "end of the world" is by adding to the verse, "or the **destruction of the wicked**, which is the end of the world" (Joseph Smith—Matthew 1:4; emphasis added, see also footnotes including D&C 45:22).

Now it is clear that this phrase is an idiom and knowing its meaning, it fits very well with what else Matthew reported that Jesus taught, as well as the other fifteen times the idiom appears throughout the scriptures. Matthew wrote, "So shall it be at the end of the world: the angels shall come forth, and sever the wicked from among the just" (Matthew 13:49).

There are calamities about which to worry, but our only worry about the "end of the world" is to make certain we are not among the wicked.

"east wind"

When Joseph was brought out of prison and given the challenge to interpret the dream of Pharaoh in Egypt, he was told the following elements of the dream:

> 22 And I saw in my dream, and, behold, seven ears came up in one stalk, full and good:
>
> 23 And, behold, seven ears, withered, thin, and **blasted with the east wind**, sprung up after them:
>
> 24 And the thin ears devoured the seven good ears: and I told this unto the magicians; but there was none that could declare it to me.
>
> 25 And Joseph said unto Pharaoh, The dream of Pharaoh is one: God hath shewed Pharaoh what he is about to do.

26 The seven good kine are seven years; and the seven good ears are seven years: the dream is one.

27 And the seven thin and ill favoured kine that came up after them are seven years; and the seven empty ears **blasted with the east wind** shall be seven years of famine." (Genesis 41:22–27; emphasis added)

To those who lived in Palestine as well as the land of the Nile River, an east wind came from the Arabian Desert. Such winds bring destruction of crops and death to man and animal who must endure the wind out of the east. Wind from the west in this area means moisture and cool from off the Mediterranean Sea.

The Book of Mormon contains two instances of the use of this idiom. Both are warnings to the people to live righteously. They are, "And again he saith: If my people shall sow filthiness they shall reap the **east wind**, which bringeth immediate destruction" (Mosiah 7:31; emphasis added), and, "And it shall come to pass that I will send forth hail among them, and it shall smite them; and they shall also be smitten with the **east wind**; and insects shall pester their land also, and devour their grain" (Mosiah 12:6; emphasis added).

It is interesting to find this idiom, which is specific to Palestine and the Middle East, used in the Book of Mormon record written on the American continent. Some would use it as an accusation that the record is a fabrication. However, others see it as another wonderful testimonial point that the record is exactly what it says it is. It is a record of a people who came to the American continent from Palestine, bringing with them their culture and idioms. Someone fabricating such a record would not likely be aware of the drastic effects of the east wind in Palestine. The Book of Mormon was first published in New England. East winds there would have meant something totally different than they did in the Middle East. This idiom was brought with these people just like idioms such as "mad hatter" and "cross the channel" came with the immigrants from Europe to America.

"followed the star"

Every Christmas in many homes the story is told to believing children that a star moved through the heavens and traveled outside its regular solar course to lead the wise men to where the Savior was born. It doesn't take them to Bethlehem, but they go to Jerusalem and are

175

told by King Herod's priests that Bethlehem was the place where the Messiah was prophesied to be born. The account regarding the wise men reads;

> 9 When they had heard the king, they departed; and, lo, the star, which they saw in the east, **went before them**, till it came and stood over where the young child was.
>
> 10 When they **saw the star**, they rejoiced with exceeding great joy.
>
> 11 And when they were come into the house, they saw the young child with Mary his mother, and fell down, and worshipped him: and when they had opened their treasures, they presented unto him gifts; gold, and frankincense, and myrrh. (Matthew 2:9–11; emphasis added)

We know that a new star appeared at the birth of the Savior. It was one of the signs to all who watched the heavens for celestial messages. Samuel foretold that not only would a new star appear, but that there would be a day and a night and a day with no darkness for his people to observe (see Helaman 14:5).

The wise men were not there the night the infant was born. Verse 11 calls him a "young child" and that they were in a house, not a stable when the wise men arrived. They had traveled from their homeland (the East), thus allowing the passage of time for the infant to become a young child and the family to be moved into a house. The account says that the star which they saw in the East, "went before them, till it came and stood over where the young child was."

If the wise men were literally following a moving star, doesn't it seem odd that the wise men went to Jerusalem and not to Bethlehem. Whomever controlled the star was not a mortal and surely had knowledge of where the child was. One phrase that causes us to believe the star moved is the idiomatic expression "went before them." If someone asked you how you had such an easy time at your large university and you answered, "All my brothers went before me. I even lived in the same apartment complex as they did. I had many of the same professors as well," does your statement have to be taken literally?

Regarding the phrase "it came and stood over," raises the question of why did Herod's servants have to "search" (v. 8)? Why didn't they just follow the same moving star? Further, why didn't everyone follow the moving star?

If you are asked further regarding your college experience, "How did you decide to become a computer animator?" Your reply might be, "I took an aptitude test and it pointed me right to that area." Should it be taken literally that the test pointed? If your uncle tells you that he is going to see you through the costly expenses of your education, does that mean he will always be watching you literally? If someone says that they have followed their dream, what does that mean? Matthew and all the prophets wrote figuratively. Furthermore, we speak and write the same way today.

Matthew was trying to show throughout his entire testimony that Jesus was the fulfillment of messianic prophecies. That included watching for the signs of the Messiah's birth and knowing the clues as to where they could find the Messiah. The Magi did rather well! They didn't need a moving star any more than a person needs a moving star today to find the Lord's Zion. If a person can't differentiate between the literal and the figurative, how will that person respond when you tell him that your feet are just killing you, or that your interview today was murder? In addition to that, those who interviewed you could see right through you and that the whole thing was a stab in the back and a slap in the face. In scripture reading as well, one should be able to tell the difference between what is to be taken literally and what is to be taken figuratively.

"upon eagles' wings"

Those who have observed the natural movements of eagles have noted that adult eagles can help young eaglets, which are learning to fly, as well as injured companions, by letting them "draft" and follow in the air that flows off the strong wings of the one bird and provides "lift" for those less strong. Note the great message the Lord gives in the following: "And again, I say unto you that it is my will that my servant Lyman Wight should continue in preaching for Zion, in the spirit of meekness, confessing me before the world; and I will bear him up as on **eagles' wings**; and he shall beget glory and honor to himself and unto my name" (D&C 124:18; emphasis added).

The Lord gives that same message to holders of the priesthood when he says, "And he shall be led in paths where the poisonous serpent cannot lay hold upon his heel, and he shall mount up in the imagination of his thoughts as upon **eagles' wings**" (D&C 124:99; emphasis added).

The Lord indicated his great help to the children of Israel in the wilderness when he said, "Ye have seen what I did unto the Egyptians, and how I bare you on **eagles' wings**, and brought you unto myself" (Exodus 19:4; emphasis added).

Then God makes a wonderful promise to all. Isaiah fashions this promise for God as he writes in his testimony, "But they that wait upon the Lord shall renew their strength; they shall mount up with **wings as eagles**; they shall run, and not be weary; [and] they shall walk, and not faint" (Isaiah 40:31; emphasis added). If we miss this idiom, how do we ever understand the message of the moving love song entitled "The Wind Beneath My Wings"?

"neither root nor branch"

This idiom was used by the Prophet Malachi. The Savior used the same words as he taught the Nephites and he attributed them to Malachi. In the latter days, the Savior also spoke the same warning for elders to use as they preached the gospel to the inhabitants of the earth. "And also that which was written by the prophet Malachi: For, behold, the day cometh that shall burn as an oven, and all the proud, yea, and all that do wickedly, shall be stubble; and the day that cometh shall burn them up, saith the Lord of hosts, that it shall leave them **neither root nor branch**" (D&C 133:64; emphasis added; see also Malachi 4:1; 3 Nephi 25:1).

What does the idiom mean? If you grow crops, you know that you will not perpetuate the life of the plant if the plant does not have roots, neither any branches to use for grafting or branches that will bear blossoms and eventually fruit. If there is no fruit, there cannot be seeds. The Lord is declaring in this idiom that the wicked will not have an inheritance nor will they have a posterity to whom they could pass anything. His words seem to speak more of not having any increase than about punishment.

"shall be as stubble" 1 Nephi 22:15

This idiom seems to always be used with the idea of readiness for destruction, that the harvest is over and preparations for plowing and preparing the soil are the next operations. However, the cycles of plowing, planting, growing, and harvesting are not negative in their nature. They are just the opposite. They are the processes of production and regeneration. The plant matures, is harvested, and then there is no fruit or seed for continued growth. That is the message of being labeled as stubble. It is the same for the Lord's statement regarding perennials, that they will not be perpetuated if they have no root or branch. The stubble is the remainder of annuals. When the harvest occurs, the root is dead and it gives no further growth and nourishment to the plant or its fruit. The plants are not considered stubble until after the harvest is over. The warning to the wicked is, "For after today cometh the burning—*this is speaking after the manner of the Lord*—for verily I say, tomorrow all the proud and they that do wickedly shall be as stubble; and I will burn them up, for I am the Lord of Hosts; and I will not spare any that remain in Babylon" (D&C 64:24; emphasis added).

The italicized statement within the verse just cited leads us to understand the events Moroni rehearsed to Joseph Smith. Moroni spoke of several unfulfilled prophecies, one of which was, "For behold, the day cometh that shall burn as an oven, and all the proud, yea, and all that do wickedly shall burn **as stubble**; for they that come shall burn them, saith the Lord of Hosts, that it shall leave them **neither root nor branch**" (Joseph Smith—History 1:37; emphasis added).

It is important to know something about what the Lord said. When he speaks of burning, he is not speaking as much about actual fire as he is speaking about having no life in the future—no growth and no seed! Stubble has no future. Without root nor branch, without seed to drop for regeneration, it is the end of its creation. That is the doom of the wicked. It is the same as stubble being burned.

These idioms sometimes confuse the uninformed. But they can be understood if we do not get misled by the literal. As idioms, their meaning is amplified, illustrated, and made more poignant when they are considered in the figurative sense. Today some of us know what it would be like to be up a creek without a paddle, to be a kite with no string, or a ship without a rudder. Our Savior stated that "the foxes have holes, and the birds of the air have nests; but the Son of man hath not where to lay his head" (Matthew 8:20). A literal take on Jesus' words would cause one to ask, "Didn't he have places where he slept? I thought he had friends." But figuratively, our Savior was saying much more. This is speaking after the manner of the Lord, and our challenge is to understand.

"take it by the tail"

Those who handle snakes know that if you hold a snake up off the ground, you basically render it unable to strike you. That is because the snake is accustomed to pushing off the ground from its coiled position in order to deliver its head and fangs to its target. It is the most successful method of overcoming and defeating a venomous snake. The Lord told Moses, "Put forth thine hand, and take it by the tail. And he put forth his hand, and caught it, and it became a rod in his hand" (Exodus 4:4).

When this verse is read, it is so natural to conclude that the Lord was telling Moses to take hold of a snake. But if we look at this verse in context, we note that the conversation was regarding Moses' problem of securing a release of the Israelite nation from the firm grasp of Egyptian power. Therefore the Lord in affect said to Moses, in figurative terms, "take this thing that you fear—going before Pharaoh, by the tail." Take away its power and it shall be a "rod" in your hand. A rod is used to rule with or to measure by. And we note in the story told in Exodus that Moses did just that. He took away the power of Pharaoh and had power over Pharaoh, and Pharaoh was measured by Moses and by God and found to be disobedient and ruled by other gods. In addition to having power over the Pharaoh and Egypt, Moses and the people who followed him, had great power over those they faced as they moved toward conquest of the promised land. They all feared Israel because Moses had conquered Egypt, and he had done it by taking his problem "by the tail."

Today similar idioms could include, "Grab the bull by the horns;" "He has his hand around my throat;" "He put me right on the chopping block all by himself;" "She put a dagger right through my heart." None of these idioms are literal. They, however, communicate messages that are explicit. They also paint a picture of the situation by using just a few words. That is the power of idioms. The only way they do not project that power is if the hearer or reader takes them literally.

"wink with their eyes"

King David was the author of most of the Psalms. However, we know that one of the psalms was written later, and according to the eastern text of the Bible, it was sung at the time Jeremiah was accused by false prophets and put into prison. It reads: "Let not them that are mine enemies wrongfully rejoice over me: neither let them wink with the eye that hate me without a cause" (Psalms 35:19 see also vv. 11, 26). Jeremiah was known as a rebel prophet because he did not agree with the false court prophets who had misled Zedekiah, the king of Judah, by their dangerous foreign policy. The last portion of the verse in the eastern text reads: "they **wink with their eyes** but they do not salute." The author was saying that they do not say, "Peace be unto you," as was the custom of easterners, when meeting. Enemies, however, did not salute, but winked with their eyes or nodded their head as a gesture of hatred. What is meant by a wink today? It can mean attraction, disdain, or a joke. The words are the same on the page but the meaning is now the reverse.

"blossom as the rose"

To read these four words as an idiom changes their meaning so much, as opposed to reading them simply as a verb and a following phrase. Discerning the meaning of the author begins by asking if the phrase is an adjective or a proverb. Is the word *blossom* a noun or a verb? Reading all the words in their setting will show that blossom is a verb. It shows action. Therefore, the phrase "as the rose" must be adverbial. It shows how, when, or where.

So something is going to blossom as the rose blossoms. Many interpret this phrase as telling of something that is going to look like the rose. However, that does not tell us how, when, or where this will happen. So, how does a rose blossom? Why does not the phrase say as a tulip, a pansy, or a sunflower? There must be something unique about a rose. If so, it can be used as a symbol. So can you identify what is unique about a rose? The Lord said, "But before the great day of the Lord shall come, Jacob shall flourish in the wilderness, and the Lamanites shall blossom as the rose" (D&C 49:24).

We want to know what we are being told by the Lord regarding the Lamanites as well as Jacob. It is so easy to think of Lamanites in the wilderness. However, the Lord seldom used words like desert and wilderness to indicate lands that lacked water or vegetation. Rather he referred to a lack of righteousness and gospel light or spiritual nourishment. In fact, the designation of being Lamanites may well refer to those who do not believe in Christ. If these elements are so, then the blossoming mentioned, must not refer to appearance as much as it does action.

While speaking to Spanish-speaking Saints in the conference center, Elder Merrill J. Bateman of the Presidency of the Seventy, said, "It was Joseph Smith who said the church would blossom across the globe. The church founder also knew of the many who would be receptive to the church's message in Latin America."[1]

Roses are unique, not just because they can be observed to move into the bud stage. But they are different because when they have buds, it is thought that they will have beautiful pedals appear very soon, just like the other flowers that form buds of one kind or another. Fruit bushes or trees immediately turn their blossoms into small, observable fruit within just days. Other flowers transform their buds and blossoms into fragrance and beauty in similar periods of time. However, the rose is distinctive. It can stay in the bud stage for weeks!

A gardener can lose patience watching rosebuds, thinking they are never going to reveal their colors and become flowers of beauty and fragrance. Often it is after the gardener has lost patience and quit watching those buds every day that he comes upon the rose bush and notices it has burst into partial bloom. Other flowers have gone from bud to full blossom in a day or so, but the rose? No, even after it has begun to open, it takes days to come into full bloom. This does not take away from its value or beauty. Roses are even shared as special gifts while in the bud stage so the recipient can enjoy the process. They can enjoy the gift and the promise it portrays.

So the idiom, "blossom as the rose" is a wonderful description for the Lamanites, who will come into the bud stage, and then all will wonder when they are ever going to flower and become magnificent. The same is true for Jacob, or Israel. Just because we observe the color and the bud beginning to show forth in a world of unbelief and unrighteousness, we should not expect it to be in bloom as soon as other prophesied events.

Isaiah used the same imagery regarding the Kingdom of Judah in his day. He wrote, "The wilderness and the solitary place shall be glad for them; and the desert shall rejoice, and blossom as the rose" (Isaiah 35:1). Many read this promise in error and expect that the physically barren places must become like flower gardens. Utah and the area called Deseret have been prophesied to blossom as a rose, but the aridness of the region has not diminished. However, what was barren regarding righteousness has become a productive garden.

The beautiful products from this former wilderness now influence the majority of the whole earth. Watching missionaries depart and return, watching conference participants, and experiencing broadcasts of the living water springing up as wells from which the thirsty may be nourished, is a wonder to behold. The wilderness certainly has begun to blossom as a rose.

It is a beautiful, thrilling, and reassuring time watching Judah, Israel, and the Lamanites go through periods wherein many say, "They will never break forth into bursting glory and fulness!" But anyone helping the master gardener will say assuredly, "Just wait. Be patient. Do not give up hope. For God's promises are sure and will all come to pass according to their own season and order. These are roses, not pansies. They will one day be in full bloom, and it will probably occur when inexperienced gardeners least expect it."

"my jewels"

Jewels are generally considered precious because of their financial worth or durability. While that may be true, there is another specialty and function for which jewels are distinguished. It is their ability to reflect light. Even common glass has been formed into crystals that imitate jewels, and when hung near candles and on chandeliers they receive the light, then magnify, dispense, and project it into realms far beyond the reach of the light they received initially. Their brilliance is not inherent. The beauty of a jewel is how it reflects the light which enters its prisms. That is when the richness, brilliance, and color is made known. In and of itself, a jewel is just another stone. But when it receives light, then it becomes something most desirable. God compares souls to jewels. What gives souls worth? "And they shall be mine, saith the Lord of Hosts, in that day when I make up **my jewels**; and I will spare them as a man spareth his own son that serveth him" (3 Nephi 24:17; emphasis added). This was said to the Nephites, letting them know how precious they were to God.

During the Restoration, the Lord declared, "For I, the Lord, rule in the heavens above, and among the armies of the earth; and in the day when I shall make up **my jewels**, all men shall know what it is that bespeaketh the power of God" (D&C 60:4; emphasis added).

Prior to the Savior coming to mortality he said, "And they shall be mine, saith the Lord of hosts, in that day when I make up **my jewels**;

and I will spare them, as a man spareth his own son that serveth him" (Malachi 3:17; emphasis added).

This idiom causes us to reflect on the question of how much of the light of God is reflected, magnified, and intensified through our personal living. It is a question that is as lasting as the jewels that we wear and which we often hold up to the light and examine. I hope there is brilliance and beauty to be observed in our lives.

Notes

1. Merrill J. Bateman, as quoted in *Deseret Morning News*, 20 Sep. 2005.

SUMMARY

The value of this book will be measured by an increased ability to identify figurative expressions in scriptural language as well as in speech. I hope you will also experience increased enjoyment when you are taught by someone who creates mental images and feelings by using metaphors and idioms.

Your awareness of how people must have been drawn to Jesus because of his skillful use of powerful, moving patterns of speech should also expand. You will notice how naturally Jesus spoke to the people who had questions in their lives. Such people as the Samaritan woman at the well in addition to his own disciples. He often spoke metaphorically. He "cut to the chase" and "pulled no punches" when the situation called for "a firm hand on the wheel."

All who desire learning should determine to ask more or better questions. Questions lead to answers. We generally wish for answers, but without questions, we won't know an answer even if it "stared us right in the face."

I hope this collection of expressions is helpful. Its completion is the culmination of years of listening, watching, and learning. But it is "only a drop in the bucket" or "the tip of the iceberg."

Last, I hope this publication has been pleasing to God. I have written for his glory and cherish his mercy and tender kindness. I hope it is also something my children will cherish and value deeply.

*The author wished to acknowledge a dear friend for his help: Writing a book is like "scaling the rock face alone without a safety rope." But I've had someone who's "over the Hill," who has cheered my every move forward. He's not just any "Tom, Dick, or Harry."

185

APPENDIX

MODERN IDIOMS

The following list of modern idioms is included to show how common such expressions are, even in modern English.

A

a quart low
a Madonna
a stud
a book worm
a computer bug
a jock
ace up his sleeve
all washed up
all he's done all his life was push
    numbers
an arm and a leg
as the crow flies
ask for her hand in marriage
asleep before my head hit the
    pillow
asleep at the switch

B

back seat driver

back stairs of the white house
bad egg
bag this
barefoot and pregnant
battle of the sexes
beach front property in Arizona
bear market
behind the eight ball
bend over backwards
big as a barn
bite your tongue
bitten by the gambling bug
blood on his hands
blossom as a rose
blue states and red states
blue in the face
bluer than blue
born with a silver spoon in his
    mouth
both candidates were slinging
    mud

bull market
bury the hatchet
busier than a one-armed paper
    hanger
by the skin of my teeth

C

can sniff out the end zone
can't win without losing
can't get over it
carbon copy
changing of the guard
chill out
cleaned his clock
clear as mud
clear as a bell
climb the walls
close the door on me
cook the books
come out of it smelling like a rose
coming in on a wing and a prayer
crystal clear
cut me some slack
cut through the red tape
cut to the chase

D

day late and a dollar short
deader than a door nail
died with his boots on
don't be a jackass
don't fence me in
don't bad mouth me
don't count your chickens before
    they hatch
don't boil over
down the road
down in the mouth

draped all over him
drink the bitter cup
drinking up all the profits
drop a dime on him
dumb like a fox
dust devil

E

eat crow
eat your heart out
eat his own words
eat my dust
end of the world
everyone knocks, but there's no
    one home.
everything he touches turns to
    gold
everything he says is a fish story
everything she says is sugar
    coated

F

feel it in my bones
fell on my face
filled with lead
fuller's soap

G

get busted
get in his face
get down and dirty
get plastered
get your act together
get stoned
get the hang of things
get the lead out
get your nose out of joint
get this project off the ground

give an inch and they take a mile
give my right arm for that
go jump in the lake
God certainly smiled upon him
going down in flames
got stood up
got a hot hand
grass won't grow under his feet
green all over
green as grass

H

hang it in your ear
Hatfields and the McCoys
have a shark attack
having a blue Monday
he was streaking
he cut his own throat
he just kept us in stitches all
    night
he is in a jam
he was feeding everyone the bull
he had to eat crow on that deal
he has good hands
he got fired
he has soft hands
he blew his money
he said that on the air
he has a nose for the ball
he has an eye for the game
he just parrots back anything you
    say
he walks on water
he blew my doors off
he was just fishing for clues
he blew his stack
he couldn't exist without blue
    tooth

he lost his shirt
he was in the house until they
    finally voted him out
he makes mountains out of
    molehills
he cried wolf
he sat on the bench most of his
    life
he bought the farm
he gave me a thumb's up
he ran off at the mouth
he bleeds blue
he has a glass chin
he was feeding us a line
he doesn't have a stomach for this
he could shake the whole town
    by lifting just one finger.
he laid the lumber to him
he gave me two bits
he has egg all over his face
he posted goose eggs
he had the key to her heart.
he carries his feelings on his
    sleeve
he always gets his piece of the pie
he is in a pickle
he drank himself into the grave
he can't carry a tune in a bucket
he has deep pockets
he looks down his nose on every-
    thing
he gave me a buck
he had me for lunch
he is a road hog
he ate my lunch
he bought the judge
he'd give you the shirt off his
    back

189

he'll flip out
he'll go into orbit
he'll go through the roof
he'll have a cow
he'll blow his stack.
he'll come through it all smelling
    like a rose
he'll blow a gasket
he'll be there until hell freezes
    over
he'll come unglued
he's a shoo-in
he's got an eye for the ball
he's just blowing smoke
he's in seventh heaven.
he's a silver-tongued fox
he's at the top of his game
he's got a mean streak a mile long
he's got sawdust for a brain
he's a dead eye
he's got a hot hand
he's got a green thumb
he's got the devil inside him
he's swimming upstream on this
    deal
he's got a yellow streak down his
    back.
he's one fry short of a happy meal
he's shooting blanks
he's a day late and a dollar short
    all the time
he's just a bunch of hot air
he's walking on egg shells all the
    time
he's down in the mouth
he's got a chip on his shoulder
he's up to his neck in alligators
he's over the hill

he's a squeaky wheel
he's a quack
he's got a heart of gold
he's in the dark about this
he's a dead ringer for him
he's hitting his own weight
he's on the bubble
he's been poisoned by being
    around those people
he's got blood on his hands
he's out to lunch
he's a boat without a rudder
he's a chip off the old block
he's wearing the collar
he's got a hole in his head
he's a lame duck
he's gone to water a tree
he's wide open
he's a couch potato
he's got ice water in his veins
he's a fish out of water
he's our canary in the mine
he's got his nose all bent out of
    shape
he's pushing up daisies
he's on speed
head of steam
head in the clouds
hell or high water
hello? Anybody up there?
his actions speak volumes
his glass is half full / half empty
hit the ceiling
hit the hay
hold his feet to the fire
hold your horses
holes in his pockets
holy smoke!

hook, line, and sinker
house of cards

I

I put fifty dollars on that horse
I threw my back out
I told him to sharpen his pencil if
we were to make a deal
I bit my tongue and didn't say
anything
I smell a skunk in here someplace
I can't live without you
I have worked my tail off
I have no place to hang my hat
I heard it through the grapevine.
I tip my hat to you
I got stood up
I was just horsing around
I lost my head.
I can read you like a book
I couldn't see the trees for the
forest
I worked my fingers to the bone
I'll take that off your hands
I'm all done in
I'm going to wash that man right
out of my hair
I'm on fire
I'm all thumbs today
I'm higher than a kite
I'm going to see a man about a
dog
I'm so hungry I could eat an
elephant
I'm using plastic
I've got to recharge my batteries
I've really fallen for you
I've got some ocean front prop-

erty in Arizona
I've got a cloud hanging over me.
if looks could kill, I'd be dead
if you can't take the heat, stay out
of the kitchen
in the black
in a groove
in the red
in one ear and out the other
in the nick of time
iron out our differences
it ain't over till the fat lady sings
it was a double header
it was right under your nose
it blew me away
it's cold as hell
it's hot as hell

J

Johnny on the spot
just blowing smoke
just horsing around

K

keep your shirt on
kick the bucket
knock your socks off

L

let the air out of his balloon
let the cat out of the bag
let your fingers do the walking
let's go crunch the numbers
life is a house of horrors
light in the forest
like a rug
like a one armed paper hanger
Lone Ranger

M

mad as a hatter
make no bones about it
makes your hair stand on end
making waves
making mountains out of mole-
    hills
March madness
mending fences
missed it by a mile
mountain to climb
my back is against the wall
my feet are killing me

N

nailed me down
nailed that sucker
no grass grows under her feet
not hitting on all eight
not to be sneezed at
now you're cooking with gas

O

on my mother's grave
one fry short of a Happy Meal
out of order
out to lunch
out of it
out of sight
over my dead body
over a barrel
over my dead body
over the back fence

P

painted the town red
paying through the nose

phone me on my dime
picked me clean
pick your brain
pillow talk
pinching pennies
pipe down
point the finger at me
politically correct
preaching to the choir
pressing his luck
prima donna
pull the wool over your eyes
pull up stakes
pulling out my hair
you're pulling my leg
pulling my own weight
punched his lights out
pure as the driven snow
push the bubble
push the envelope
pushing up daisies
put the cart before the horse
put your money where your
    mouth is
put the petal to the metal
put your best foot forward
put my foot in my mouth

R

rain on your parade
raise Cain
raking in the dough
ran into a brick wall
read you like a book
ripped out my heart
ripped off
rise and shine
rock solid

rode off into the sunset
roll over in his grave
run and gun
run out of steam
running on fumes

S

sand in their shoes
save your breath
saved by the bell
saw into my soul
say a word of prayer
say cheese
scoot along
see red
separate the men from the boys
set the world on fire
she slammed the door in his face
she really threw him a curve ball
she nearly had a cow
she can talk a mile a minute·
she stabbed me in the back
she really blindsided him
she makes time stand still
she gave me the evil eye
she can smell a sale a mile away
she's got eyes in the back of her
    head
she's a breath of fresh air
she's a real looker
she's the grim reaper
she's no spring chicken
she's gone to powder her nose
she's got him wrapped around
    her finger
she's a dynamite member
she's the wicked witch of the
    north

shooting fish in a barrel
shut up
silver bullet
simmer down
single handed
sink your teeth into
skating on thin ice
slick as a whistle
smell the roses
smelling like roses
sold me down the river
sold me a bill of goods
some day it will dawn on him
somebody else packed my para-
    chute
something's fishy here
son of a gun
stand by your word
stand by your guns
stand on your head
star wars
stick your neck out
stirring up the pot
stole me blind
straight from the horse's mouth
stuff this up your nose
surf the web
sweet sixteen
swept off her feet
swimming upstream
swinging in the breeze

T

talked myself blue in the face
taste of your own medicine
text me
that gave me a black eye
that was a knuckle ball

193

that's a pea-brained idea
the venom of his own anger is
    eating him alive
the basket tonight was just huge
the walls were paper thin
the price is sky high
the last straw
the judge threw the book at him
these colors don't run
they gave me lots of rope
they were making out
they got fed home cooking
they gave the bride a shower
they were upside down in their
    house
they're coming out of the wood-
    work
this deal is going right down the
    drain
this is a downer (or bummer)
this is top-drawer stuff
this car is a gas hog
this thing is crooked
this sounds rather corny
this project is starting to fly
this ain't my first time around the
    block
this idea stinks
threw me out
throw me a line
tie the knot
they were sparking
till rivers run upstream
till the stars fall from the skies
till the moon turns to silver
time was flying by
time never sleeps
took my breath away

took the words out of my mouth
tongue in cheek
tough pill to swallow
trial by fire
Trojan horse
tripped me up
turned up her nose to the deal
twenty-four seven

U

up a creek without a paddle
up against a wall

W

waiting for the other shoe to fall
walked all over me
wanna be like Mike
wasted
what a real back breaker
what he's got up his sleeve
watch every step you take
watch your back
we swept them
we follow the sun
we were playing phone tag
wet behind the ears
whale of an idea
what's good for the goose is good
    for the gander
when pigs fly
where's the fire
with a forked tongue
with one arm tied behind his
    back
wolf in sheep's clothing
written in the sand

Y

yank your chain
you are going to hell in a hand-
    basket
you light up my life
you clean up real fine
you are my sunbeam.
you could hear yourself think
you are the wind beneath my
    wings
you are what you eat
you made my day

you can just see it in his eye
you'd better sharpen your pencil
    if you want to deal with me
you'll be seeing stars
you're all wet
you're grounded
you're washed up
you're just asking for trouble
you're just shooting blanks
you're out of your tree
you've put me in a corner
your cross to bear

WHERE DID THAT COME FROM?

This section provides a few interesting tidbits that the author has gleaned over the years about some common modern idioms.

- The term "the whole nine yards" came from World War II fighter pilots in the South Pacific. When arming their airplanes on the ground, the 50-caliber machine ammo belts measured exactly twenty-seven feet before being loaded into the fuselage. If the pilots fired all their ammo at a target, it got the whole nine yards.

- Hershey's Kisses are called that because the machine that makes them looks like it's kissing the conveyor belt.

- "I'll just give this a lick and a promise," is what you might say if you only had the time or energy to quickly mop up a spill on the floor without moving any of the furniture. You give the mopping a quick effort with the promise to return and do it completely. "A lick and a promise" was an idiom that became used for doing any job partially while promising to come back in the future and do it fully.

- The phrase "rule of thumb" is derived from an old English law, which stated that you couldn't beat your wife with anything wider than your thumb.

- The name Jeep came from the abbreviation used in the army for the "General Purpose" vehicle—thus G. P.

- The nursery rhyme "Ring around the Rosies" is a rhyme about the plague. Infected people with the plague would get red circular sores ("Ring around the rosie . . ."), these sores would smell badly so common folks would put flowers on their bodies somewhere inconspicuously, so that it would cover the smell of the sores ("a pocket full of posies . . ."). People who died from the plague would be burned so as to reduce the possible spread of the disease and the airborne ashes seemed a constant element to be coming from the air ("ashes, ashes, we all fall down!")

- "Getting cold feet" was a military term used in the seventeenth century. In that time the armies of some countries were very poorly equipped, especially in regard to shoes or boots. A well-equipped general would often engage another army in the dead of winter because soldiers with cold or frozen feet would more likely retreat than those with warm feet. Thus "getting cold feet" meant to back out!

- "I heard it through the grape vine" comes to us from the Civil War. War rumors came on the grape vine telegraph, which was a reference to the fact that there were no real telegraph lines in camp to supply accurate information. The folklore is that soldiers leaving camps to go to the front lines would often attach notes on trees and vines next to the latrines. These notes contained facts relative to the war.

- "Riding piggy back" is a saying having nothing to do with pigs. It is a corruption of "pick-a-pack" which in turn came from "pick back." These terms referred to packs or sacks that people threw on their backs to carry items.

- "Indian summer" is a warm spell in fall that is not summer but is summer-like in its weather. The term comes to us the same way as "Indian giver." Both have a negative connotation wherein something is not what it appears like. The New England settlers felt this way about the Indians because they did not understanding the Native Americans and their ways.

- "God bless you!" In the middle ages, legend had it that when a person sneezed, the soul temporarily left the body (because all the breath of life was vacated). However, saying, "God bless you," prevented their soul from being snatched away by the devil.

- "Get someone's goat." This phrase came from the practice of putting a goat inside a skittish racehorse's stall. It supposedly had a calming influence. A sly gambler might persuade a stable boy to remove the goat shortly before the race, thereby upsetting the horse and reducing its chance of winning.

- "Here's mud in your eye." This was originally said to someone you were racing on horseback. It meant that you were going to beat the person and since he would be behind you, he would catch mud flying from the wet track in his face.

- "Kit and caboodle" The Dutch word "boedel" means "effects" or what a person owns (his personal effects). Robbers adopted the term, calling whatever they stole "boodle." They carried their burglar tools in a "kit." If they were able to enter a house, gather everything valuable, and make a clean escape, they said that they had gotten away with the "kit and boodle." In time, the terms "kit" and "boodle" seemed to be combined into one term, "caboodle." The "kit" was then reintroduced into the phrase, probably for emphasis.

- "This will do in a pinch." or "I need a pinch." These phrases seem to have come from, "I'm in a pinch," or "I'm in need of a pinch." During the early days of the gold rush in California, those who found gold dust or nuggets had difficulty in spending their gold, even for supplies. Those Mormons who were among the first to find it, sent much of their gold to Utah, and there in 1849 the first gold coins were minted in Salt Lake. It was not an official mint of the US government, but that was not a concern for the Mormons. For about three years, before an agent was sent to California, those with gold dust transacted business in a variety of ways. Besides sending their gold to the East to be minted, they traded with it. In a saloon, the price of a drink became the amount of gold dust the bartender could "pinch" between his thumb and forefinger. It became common for bartenders to be hired for the size of their hands or the width of their fingers and thumb. Hence, "a pinch will do."

- Where did the phrase "private eye" come from? In the times of the Pinkerton Detectives, they had a phrase on their logo which said, "We never blink." This meant that nothing escaped their observation in their pursuit of those who broke the law. Out of this concept came the profession of individual investigators who would follow the concept of the Pinkertons. They were not with any agency, they were "private eyes."

- "Treated like chopped liver." It is believed the phrase was originally coined in America. Since chopped liver was always considered a side dish and not a main course, the phrase is used to express hurt and amazement when a person feels he has been overlooked or tossed to the side.

- Before kitchens and smaller cooking vessels, cooking was generally done with a big kettle that always hung over or near the fire. Every day, they lit the fire and added things to the pot. They ate mostly vegetables and did not get much meat. They would eat the stew for dinner, leaving leftovers in the pot to get cold overnight, and then start over the next day. Sometimes the stew had food in it that had been there for quite awhile—hence the rhyme, "peas porridge hot, peas porridge cold, peas porridge in the pot nine days old."

- "Not worth a tinker's dam." A tinker was a craftsman who navigated city streets and country roads in a horse-drawn cart, offering his services to mend pots and pans by repairing broken handles, smoothing dents, and especially repairing small holes. The latter involved fashioning a moist clay dam around the hole. Then as he blocked its interior with a thick pad of leather or asbestos, he would pour a small amount of solder into the dam. The solder cooled almost immediately and the tinker could brush or wash away the now worthless dam. Perhaps this phrase applies to Clark Gable's "Frankly, my dear, I don't give a dam!" Maybe he was not swearing!

- At one time only the wealthy had slate floors or something other than dirt, hence the saying "dirt poor." These slate floors would get slippery in the winter, when wet, so they spread straw that had been threshed or another plant material onto the floor to help keep their footing and collect the soil. As the winter wore on, they kept adding more thresh until when you opened the door it would all start slipping outside. To fix this problem a piece of wood was placed in the entry way—hence, a "thresh hold."

- Regarding money: The term "buck" dates back around 1740 when deer hides were traded. A dollar was the going price. The term "dough" became used around 1851. It emphasized paper currency's role as one of life's necessities. "Dollar" derived from the Germanic "thaler" used throughout Europe and Britain from the 1500s to the 1700s to refer to large silver coins. The English translation was "dollar." "Sawbuck" was a name of an early sawhorse with legs that crossed to form an X, the Roman numeral for 10, or a $10 bill. "Grand" is short for "grand amount," which at the time in the early 1920s was $1,000.

- Why are some towns called "Jerk water towns?" Answer: When early steam engines ran dry at a town without a water tower, the crew had to "jerk" water in buckets from wells and haul it to the locomotive. Hence, they contemptuously labeled the place a "jerk water town."

- Why is A&W Root Beer so named? Answer: It is for Agnes and Willard Marriott. They started the A&W business before they went into the hotel business.

- How is "kicking the bucket" associated with death? Answer: The method of killing pigs, which gave rise to the expression, has long since died out. Long ago in Norfolk, England, a pig was killed by raising the live pig by its hind legs from a beam. In this position, its throat was slit. The nervous reflex actions of the pig, after its throat was cut, sometimes made it difficult to catch the blood in a receptacle, generally a bucket. The thrashing of the animal caused it to often kick the bucket as it was dying.

- Lead cups were used to drink ale or whiskey. The combination would sometimes knock people out for a couple of days, making them appear dead. Also, during times of plague or disease, sick people who showed no signs of life such as a discernible pulse or detectable breathing were often treated as dead and prepared for burial. The body needed to be protected from insects and vermin but also observed for any signs of recovery and life, so the body was usually observed for a couple of days. Family members would gather and wait to see if the corpse would wake up—hence the custom of holding a "wake."

- At one time, pewter was the favored choice for plate and cup material, if you could afford it. Food with a high acid content caused some of the lead in the pewter to leach into the food, causing lead poisoning and death. This happened most often with tomatoes, so, for the next four hundred years or so, tomatoes were considered poisonous. Others in Europe simply avoided tomatoes because they resembled foods thought to be poisonous.

- At one time it was the custom to divide a loaf of bread amongst the members of a household according to status. Workers got the burnt bottom of the loaf, the wealthy family members got the rest, except for when a sovereign was present. Then it was customary to slice the top portion off the bread and present it to the ranking guests at the table. This eventually led to calling the elite, who were offered this choicest portion, the "upper crust."

- During wintertime before running water and hot water heaters were staples in homes, baths for the family consisted of a big tub filled with hot water. The same water was used by the entire family. The adults of the house had the privilege of the most clean water, then the children, last of all the babies. By then, the water was so dirty you could actually lose someone in it—hence the hyperbole, "Don't throw the baby out with the bath water."

- Why would someone, particularly from the Southwest, say, "We've howdyed, but we ain't shook yet?" Answer: They are telling you that you've met, but haven't been formally introduced.

- What does someone mean if they say, "She's got tongue enough for ten rows of teeth?" They are telling you that she's a real talker.

- In Western language, if you want to say that you are not a novice, but have "been around," you might say, "This ain't my first rodeo."

INDEX OF IDIOMS

INDEX OF SCRIPTURES CITED

NEW TESTAMENT

BOOK OF MORMON

DOCTRINE AND COVENANTS

ABOUT THE AUTHOR

George M. Peacock grew up in Orangeville, Utah. He has sought answers to scriptural questions throughout his life, beginning with his service as a full-time missionary to Independence, Missouri. His area of labor later included much of the Bible Belt.

After his mission he earned a bachelor's degree in secondary education and a master's degree in religious education, both from Brigham Young University. He began teaching seminary and institute classes in 1964, retiring in 2000. In addition to teaching he fulfilled assignments in both administration and teacher improvement.

George married Arlene Christensen of Meridian, Idaho, in 1963. They are the parents of five married children who reside near them in St. George, Utah.